WHERE WERE YOU
WHEN I NEEDED YOU
DAD?

WHERE WERE YOU WHEN I NEEDED YOU DAD?

A GUIDE FOR HEALING YOUR FATHER WOUND

Jane Myers Drew, Ph.D.

Tiger Lily Publishing

Newport Beach, California

Workshops and Lectures

Jane Myers Drew, Ph.D., offers workshops and educational programs about healing the father-wound. She also gives training seminars for mental health professionals. For a schedule of upcoming lectures, workshops, and seminars, or if you are interested in bringing a program to your area, please write to her at the address below.

The author welcomes any responses to *Where Were You When I Needed You, Dad?*

Dr. Jane Myers Drew
c/o Tiger Lily Publishing
P.O. Box 15277
Newport Beach, CA 92659
(949) 645-5907

Grateful acknowledgment is made for the lyrics to "Insulated," copyright © 1989 by Randy Eliopulos. Reprinted by permission of the author. The anonymous originators of the wise sayings that appear in the special emphasis boxes also deserve recognition.

Copy Editing: David Lionel, Ralph Fairweather, Candi Dabney, Nicole Conte
Cover: Lynn Knipe
Lay-out: Rich Governali

Library of Congress Catalog Card Number: 91-068455

ISBN 1-880883-00-7

For my father, Stephen George Myers,
who gave me life. Even though I barely knew him,
he left me a legacy of kindness and gentleness to guide and comfort me,

for my mother, Bernadette Gales Myers,
who was both mother and father to me,

and for my friend, David Lionel,
whose support and energy provided the inspiration
and activating force that kept me going to complete this book.

ACKNOWLEDGEMENTS

I am delighted to acknowledge all the help I have received. I had three principal editors. Foremost was David Lionel, who gave profusely of himself and his time. He constantly challenged me to depth of thought and clarity of expression. Ralph Fairweather offered invaluable feedback, especially on structure and the organization of material. Candi Dabney provided fresh ideas and a tone of familiarity that increased the text's readability. All of these people were incredibly patient in helping me make improvements throughout the book's numerous stages. I appreciate their support and the team spirit we shared in doing this project.

I am especially grateful to my clients and the students in my classes, who shared their stories, rich insights, and touching drawings. Special kudos to Jane Carter for her supplemental illustrations. Thanks are also due to my family, friends, and colleagues, who encouraged me many times during the long birthing process. Sharon Roy, Virginia Foster, and Maurice Ogden generously read and critiqued the manuscript. Lyda Hill steered me toward the concept of producing a workbook in the first place.

I've had many mentors along my path, who have contributed their ideas and inspired me with the wisdom and devotion they bring to their work. Some were personal teachers, while others gave workshops I attended or authored books that influenced me. They include Elyce Wakerman, William Erwin, Barbara De Angelis, John Bradshaw, Shakti Gawain, Russ Read, David Viscott, Steve Winer, Harold Bloomfield, Robert Bly, Larry Hedges, Virginia Wink Hilton, Lee Holloway, Karen Jenkins, Linda Schierse Leonard, Emily Coleman, Susan Christopher, Brugh Joy, and Robert Kent Myers.

I deeply thank them all.

Jane Myers Drew
Newport Beach, California

CONTENTS

INTRODUCTION

How many of the following statements could apply to you?

- "I seldom think of my father without feeling sad or angry."

- "I expect too much of myself – and probably of others as well."

- "I am confused about my role as a man."

- "I lack confidence in my femininity."

- "I'm afraid that people I love will leave me."

- "I feel fearful frequently. I've developed a 'safe' life in order to avoid risks."

- "I have had a difficult time breaking away from my mother's influence to become my own person."

- "I lack discipline and direction in my life."

- "I feel either defiant or weak around authority figures."

- "I have difficulty making decisions. I don't trust myself."

- "When I'm close to success, something seems to hold me back from it."

- "I can't seem to make intimate relationships work for me."

- "I wonder if I'll ever be satisfied with myself."

Do you recognize yourself in any of these descriptions? If so, it is likely that you suffer from a father-wound. When you were growing up, you may not have had the quantity or quality of fathering you needed. Experiencing the loss of your father's love or involvement, or perhaps enduring his abuse, could have left you scarred.

As a psychologist and workshop leader, I conduct seminars all over North America that help people focus on their relationships with their fathers. Most participants describe their dads as a far cry from the protective, guiding, nurturing man portrayed in *Father Knows Best*. Instead, their memories reflect pain, humiliation, fear, and resentment. Here are a few of their stories.

"My only remembrance of childhood is my dad teasing me about my ears that stuck out. I felt so ashamed, especially when he did it in front of my older brother."

"My father would yell in anger at dinner every night. Often, for no reason, he would blow up and hit me."

"I'm thirty-two, and I've never met my father. My mother got pregnant out of wedlock. My father had no interest in getting married. He was horrified at the thought of a child. Then I had a step-father for a year and a half when I was six. He was distant and abusive. Fathers don't hold much charm for me."

"My father is an active alcoholic. He's been emotionally and physically abusive my whole life. He molested my half sister, who's five years older than I. This has just come to light in the last two years."

* All the drawings in this book are by father-wound workshop participants. They used their non-dominant hands to get in touch with intense childhood feelings about their dads.

"My dad was a nice person who provided well for us. He just spent every minute at home in front of the TV. He'd come to the breakfast table with a little radio to listen to the morning news. He'd hardly say a word through dinner. All evening he'd be in front of the TV with the newspaper on his lap. If I asked him a question, he wouldn't even answer."

I am always touched by these sad tales. Most workshop members seem amazed to discover how many other people have experienced serious problems with their fathers. Unfortunately, such traumas are all too common.

Do you find yourself in any of these stories? Perhaps yours is different but equally painful. Whatever the specifics, your father-wound is most likely affecting your life right now. A child experiences a major, life-altering loss whenever a father dies, lives apart because of divorce or abandonment, or is absent from home a great deal due to travel or the military. A youngster's critical needs for fathering are also not met when dad is present in the house but is emotionally distant, judgmental, physically or sexually abusive, or is addicted to work or substances.

One seminar attendee shared a song he had written describing how he keeps himself emotionally isolated. When he was just eight, his parents had a fight, after which his father left for good, without even talking to the little boy. Now as a grown man, he knows he has a damaged and scared child inside that he tries to ignore.

> **I'm insulated, nobody gets a grip on me**
> **Sophisticated, nobody's going to rip on me**
> **I'm insulated, nobody's going to hurt me now**
>
> **Life from a distance seems safer somehow**
> **Time to think and time to react**
> **No regretting what you might have said**
> **No wishing you could take your words back**
>
> **When my wife asked me, "Why are you so cold?**
> **If I touch you, would you even bleed?"**
> **I told her, "Don't take it personally,**
> **I just stay ready for the day that you'll leave."**
>
> **I remember the fighting, still hear the glass break**
> **Mama screamed until she cried**
> **Mama broke the news in a roundabout way**
> **And Daddy never told me good-bye**
>
> **But I was a good little eight year-old boy**
> **Choked back my frights and my fears**
> **I've never fussed, and I've never cried**
> **Now I ain't cried in twenty-five years**

> **Sometimes late at night I hear the screams of a child**
> **From the empty bedroom upstairs**
> **But I never bother to get up and look**
> **I know there can't be anyone there**
>
> **'Cause I'm insulated, nobody gets inside of me**
> **Not loved or hated, I'm just the way I want to be**
> **Insulated, there's nobody to hurt me now**

Because a father is so important to a child's development, hurtful interactions with him keep affecting you as an adult, limiting the degree to which you value yourself, your ability to be intimate, and your success at work.

Many people have scars left from their experience with their dads. My own father-wound shaped my life, though for many years I was unconscious of just how profound the effect was. When I finally became aware of the extent of the damage, I could begin healing myself.

Hearing about my process of awakening can help you realize how significantly your relationship with your dad has influenced you. In my account of what happened to me, you will see elements we have in common, even though our particular experiences may vary.

I divide my own father-loss story into three acts. **Act One** lasted fourteen months. I was born into a normal family in Racine, Wisconsin. I had a mother, father, three older sisters, and an older brother. My dad owned a filling station and garage. My mother raised the children, gave piano lessons, and was the church organist.

 My father's heart had been weakened by childhood rheumatic fever. When I was just over a year old, he caught a cold that quickly progressed into pneumonia. Two weeks after his doctors sent him to the Mayo Clinic in Minnesota, he died of heart failure. He was only thirty-seven.

Today I understand that losing him was the most significant event in my life.

Act Two spanned from age fourteen months to my late thirties. I grew up aware that I didn't have a dad like other kids, but I thought it didn't matter very much. My mother's influence dominated me because my father wasn't there. She was as hard on her children as she was on herself. As a result, I learned to demand a lot of myself and not to take much credit when I did succeed.

In grade school, I felt left out because I didn't have a dad. I watched as my friends' fathers took them on vacations, helped them with homework, laughed with them, and held their hands. In high school, I had wild crushes on boys I barely knew. This repeated my relationship with my father... the longing, the distance, the wanting, but *never having* the contact and closeness that I desired.

In my early twenties, I was frequently depressed and afraid to make decisions. Often I had thoughts of suicide. As for romances, I had two kinds. In one, fellows would like me, but I wouldn't care for them. When they wanted to get nearer, I'd be frightened and keep my distance. In the other, I would get excited about a man who wasn't much interested in me. Choosing men who didn't return my caring allowed me to experience being "in love," followed by feeling abandoned. Whether pursued or pursuing, I ended up lonely.

In my late twenties, I became a social worker and then a psychotherapist, even though I had persistent doubts about my talent and skill. All this time, I *knew* what would make me happy and solve all my problems: getting married. In my early thirties, I finally married a man who was twelve years my senior. At the time, it never crossed my mind that I was looking for a father in him. Ultimately, in trying to please him so that he would take care of me, I gave too much of myself away. Eight years later, we divorced.

Fortunately, my dismal story has an **Act Three**! In my late thirties, I came across a book called *Father Loss* by Elyce Wakerman which helped me break through to my feelings about my father. Every story she told showed me how my pattern of chronic anguish and confusion related to losing him.

I was already in counseling, so I had a safe place to talk about my dad and cry my tears. Up to this point, when my therapist had mentioned my father, I would always say, "He's not the problem, my mother is." Now I could focus on my sad and lonely feelings about my absent father. I realized how angry I was that I had to grow up without a dad. I experienced and released my pain. I shared with friends my emotions and new insights and listened to their stories about their fathers.

Reviewing how father-loss had affected my adult life, I realized I didn't feel valuable unless I had a man to love me. I was uncomfortable in social situations because of harsh self-judgments. Much of the time, I felt guilty and ashamed. Though driven to achieve and gain recognition, I often questioned my career choice and wondered about my life's purpose.

As I healed and changed, a critical revelation came to me. If I, as a trained psychologist, had been denying the importance of my inadequate fathering, there must be many other people who also struggle with unresolved feelings about their dads. I began developing a workshop where people could learn ways to repair their father-wounds.

This guidebook has evolved from the experiences I have had interacting with thousands of men and women in these seminars on father-loss. Over the years, workshop participants have expressed their deep need and appreciation for the opportunity to heal. Just as they came to recognize how their dads impacted them, you can make links between your current problems and how your dad treated you.

Your father-wound has probably affected the most pivotal and intimate aspects of your life – your very heart and soul. If you weren't valued and loved for yourself by your dad, you may not have fully matured, like a tender sapling cut off from sunlight. By confronting your father issues, you can free yourself to find new confidence and direction. With this enhanced understanding, you too can claim the power to transform your life.

As I continue to recover from the effects of my father-loss, I gain greater confidence in myself. I don't feel desperate anymore when I'm not in a romantic relationship. I'm getting better at setting my boundaries with men so that I feel safe and respected. I socialize with greater ease and enjoyment. A pattern of insomnia that started in grade school has transformed into full nights of blessed sleep.

Above all, I have begun to accept and love myself more. I'm still evolving, yet so much more of the time now, I feel happy to be alive. I do a better job of balancing work and pleasure. I exercise at the gym and eat healthier foods. I allow myself to take more creative risks in writing, speaking, and counseling clients. I have also discovered more of my purpose in life, which includes sharing what I have learned about healing from inadequate fathering.

SEVEN STEPS TO HEALING

"Father-wound," "father-loss," and "inadequate fathering" are interchangeable terms that describe the damaging childhood experiences you had with your dad. Recovering from their effects will give you greater self-esteem. You will feel more satisfied at work and improve your capacity for intimacy. As you delve deeper inside yourself, you will even discover the positive elements in your father-loss. For it is in the painful process of grappling with adversity, discovering your true inner nature, and giving yourself permission to grow, that you experience the most aliveness!

There are seven steps you can take to heal from your father-wound and recreate your relationship with your father. First, ***increasing your awareness of dad's impact*** helps you define what you missed with your father when you were young and what you actually received from him. You get clear on your feelings toward him.

Second, ***mourning and letting go of your pain*** involves getting in touch with the hurt and anger you have long suppressed regarding your dad. Expressing your feelings is essential to healing. Powerful exercises help you release your disappointment and rage.

Third, ***reappraising your father*** begins with seeing him as a human being in his own right. Once you are ready to incorporate your father's perspective, you will understand that he only passed on to you what had been done to him. You work to forgive and even appreciate him. Saying good-bye to the dad of your youth helps you emotionally release any remaining expectations you have of him.

Fourth, ***healing the child within*** encourages you to reconnect with how the young part of you wanted to be nurtured and treasured by a tender father. You honor your little child inside by allowing desires and feelings to emerge that you denied growing up. You learn to accept and savor positive feedback.

Fifth, ***becoming your own good father*** shows you ways to fill in for the experiences you felt you missed with your dad. As a devoted father would do for his child, you can help yourself acknowledge your deepest desires and goals. When your outlook on your dad changes, so will your perspective on your "heavenly father" and the life of the spirit. Through meditative communion with nature, you can move toward a sense of the universe as benign and caring rather than hostile or indifferent. Experiencing such a loving connection will put you in touch with deep wellsprings of inner peace and strength.

Sixth, ***acknowledging the wisdom of the father-wound*** helps you accept the direction that your life has taken. You see the strengths you've developed. Finding contentment in being alone, along with achieving self-acceptance, together open the doorway into self-love.

Seventh, ***reconnecting with your dad*** completes the circle of recovery. Now that you see your father in a new light and have found your own power, you should be open to trying new ways of relating with him, whether he is alive or dead. A deeper bonding based on mutual respect may still be possible.

Once you have gone through these steps, and you understand how your father-wound affects all your interactions, you can apply what you've learned to ***building satisfying relationships***. By consciously cultivating caring mentors as father substitutes, you can experience that you are valuable and deserve support and recognition. You can carry on the healing process with those who are closest to you by going back to the original source of your upset feelings when they arise. You learn to see and nurture the little child in your loved ones, and above all to appreciate the good in them and you.

HOW TO USE THIS GUIDE

This book contains a series of exercises I have developed from my workshops on father-loss. The more you commit yourself to healing through doing these processes, the greater your assurance of positive results. I use a wide range of techniques, so be prepared to involve yourself in writing, drawing, tape recording, role-playing, and other experiences.

You can use this manual in several different ways, depending on your needs and preferences. Utilize it in a group, as an adjunct to therapy, with a buddy, or on your own. This work may stir up uncomfortable feelings. Emotional change can be difficult. Many of you have problems now because you had no one to turn to while you were growing up. To survive, you learned to isolate yourself or hide your feelings.

Why not proceed differently this time? You can create a nurturing environment where others participate in the recovery process with you. You do not have to go through it alone. Sharing what's inside you is healing. Tell your story to people who will listen and care. Let yourself cry in front of them. As the rain nurtures the ground, so too your tears nourish your being.

I strongly recommend that your father-loss healing be a joint undertaking. Collective wisdom enhances and accelerates your growth. In a ***group***, you break through the defense of keeping your pain to yourself. You get response, validation, and encouragement from others to reveal and be yourself. In my workshops, people often choke up when they talk about their dads. Their spontaneous release gives the entire gathering permission to show feelings. Each individual's open communication of his or her pain sets a tone of safety and provides a basis for mutual trust.

You can probably find others who will commit themselves to working along with you. Or you may already be in a support group which will take on this project. If there is a therapist leader, so much the better. Most of the exercises can be done during the group. Others are more effectively done at home, with a follow up discussion at the next meeting.

Investigate all the ways you can fill your emotional needs. If you want to seek *professional help*, there are many fine counselors who deal with issues from childhood. You can also check with local mental health clinics and community colleges for related *workshops*, such as one on resolving grief. *Self-help groups* like Adult Children of Alcoholics, Survivors of Incest Anonymous, or Co-Dependents Anonymous are also available throughout the country. I've included a list of contact information for support groups at the back of the book.

One of the reasons people appreciate my seminar is that it provides a structured space where they can get this internal work completed. It is often difficult to make yourself confront painful issues. If you say that you want to do the exercises, yet you don't actually get around to them, or if you feel daunted by the prospect of doing them all, an alternative to working in a group is finding a *buddy* to collaborate with you. Meet with this partner on a routine basis. Make a mutual commitment to recovery and keep each other accountable.

To do the exercises *on your own*, establish a quiet time and a private place where you can cry or shout, without fear of being criticized or disturbed. Schedule a regular appointment with yourself and determine to do whatever the exercises require.

You may choose to start by simply *reading through* parts of the text, without doing the exercises. There is great value in just going over the material. Proceed slowly, because the concepts take time to digest. This review will prepare you to go back and undertake the exercises.

Working through emotions and shifting your attitudes take time. These processes touch tender spots and require deep consideration. A good way to proceed is to practice one exercise every day or two. Most require no more than ten to fifteen minutes. A few need as much as half an hour.

One cautionary note: you may give yourself reasons to resist this healing process, such as, "I'm too bored... too busy... too sophisticated... too tired..." Acknowledge these excuses as reflecting natural fears that anyone has approaching a life-transforming venture. If you feel reluctant to try any particular exercise, you may not be ready to deal with it or just may not sense its relevance for you. On the other hand, resistance is often a sign that you are on the brink of a significant breakthrough.

It is important to go easy on yourself, respecting your own sensitivity and timing. But don't let any processes that intimidate or fail to appeal to you keep you from the ones that are appropriate for you to do.

NUTS AND BOLTS PREPARATION

To facilitate your interior explorations, you will need a **tape recorder** and **audio cassette tapes**. You will be recording yourself speaking certain exercise instructions. If you prefer, I offer pre-recorded audio tapes with much of this material prepared for you. You will find a listing of these cassettes on the order form at the back of the book. You will in any case tape your responses. Buy a number of thirty-minute cassettes, recording only one exercise per side, clearly labeled with the title and the date for future reference.

At times your inner self needs coaxing to emerge. Writing and arts and crafts are excellent means to bring out your thoughts and feelings. Start a **personal journal** to go along with this workbook, since many of the exercises ask you to answer questions or write out your reactions. A three-ring binder works well for this purpose. In journal writing, you pull another person out of yourself, permitting engagement in a kind of dialogue. There's the "you" who writes and the "you" who gains perspective by reading about yourself. You become your own companion, while gaining self-awareness.

Looking back at these cassettes and journals in the years to come will offer a clear picture of this phase in your life. You can recall the struggles you've weathered and the progress you've made. Your spoken and written words will reveal yourself at great depth.

Some of the exercises will prompt you to make **drawings,** an especially powerful tool for accessing your authentic nature. Artistic talent is not required; it may even be a distraction. You won't be drawing to measure your creative ability but to connect with your subconscious mind and get into your feelings. You can use stick figures or represent your emotions with symbols like the sun or clouds. Enjoy your imagination in action and evaluate your results charitably.

One useful hint: work with your non-dominant hand when sketching – right-handers use their left hands, left-handers their right. Utilizing your "other" hand gives you less conscious control, putting you more in contact with the basic emotions you had as a child. All the drawings that appear throughout the text were done by class members with their opposite hands. Many of them have been glad for the chance to sketch because it is an expressive activity which they rarely have permitted themselves. Making pictures can open up a lot of feelings. Unearthing your emotions leads you to "pay dirt."

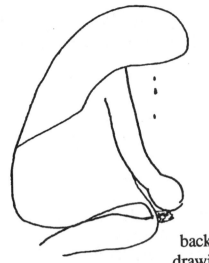

"I can draw much better with my left hand than I imagined," one surprised and elated group participant said. "Drawing evoked emotions that were closer to the surface than I thought."

"Drawing was liberating," commented another. "It got me in touch with the kid in me and made me realize my creative self was being neglected."

During my workshops, I play **soft music** in the background when participants are writing, role-playing, drawing, or imagining scenes. One class member said she remained unmoved doing an exercise at home, but when we did the same process in class with music, she cried. I recommend that you put on music that touches you when you do the work in this manual. I make available a tape called *Lazaris Remembers Lemuria* which is particularly lovely and works very well as an accompaniment to the exercises.

I will be your guide on this journey toward wholeness, doing my best to keep you on track with your emotions, while steering you clear of the pitfalls of despair and discouragement. I will continually applaud you and encourage you to complete each stage in your growth.

My hope is that you will face head on your history and feelings, confronting what may have been too difficult or frightening to deal with earlier in your life. You will need self-discipline to keep doing the exercises. It may seem easier to put this book in a drawer and retreat into the familiar refuges of anger, depression, or self-pity. From my own personal and professional experience, I know that persevering will bring invaluable rewards.

You are undertaking a heroic task. Take courage from the fact that many others have followed the same path to recover from their father-wounds. Despite your past with your dad, you deserve to have fulfillment and pleasure. As you grow, you will discover how to love and empower yourself to a greater degree. You will learn to enjoy each moment as it is and participate more fully in the mystery and wonder of being alive.

SECTION ONE

INCREASING YOUR AWARENESS OF DAD'S IMPACT

At long last, our society is beginning to recognize the tremendous impact a father has on a youngster's life. For years, the mother has received the primary focus in the child-rearing process. She has also carried the burden of the blame for problems. Of course, the mother's role is extremely important. So is the father's.

A good father protects his children by providing time and space for them to grow. He acts as a role model, balancing appropriate nurturing and discipline with play and adventure. He is a bridge to the world outside the family, encouraging his offspring to explore and take risks. A concerned father often looks beyond his own comfort to meet the needs of his youngsters. He is sensitive and flexible. He willingly accepts responsibility for helping his children realize their potential.

MIXED MEMORIES

Many men delight in their children and enjoy being fathers. Everyone has different experiences with his or her dad. To increase your awareness of what you did or did not receive from your father when you were growing up, it may help you to observe some dads in action. Watching fathers and their youngsters relate may bring up for you a mix of memories and feelings. Favorable recollections such as "We shared many pleasant family outings" may alternate with painful ones, such as "He would humiliate me in front of his friends." You may remember the good reasons you have to feel both grateful and angry.

EXERCISE 1. WATCH FATHERS AND CHILDREN

Not long ago, I went to an amusement park. I found myself noticing fathers and their little children. Once in a while, a few of the dads were impatient, insisting on taking youngsters on rides they weren't ready for, but most were very supportive. They held hands with their sons or daughters on the way to the ride and hung onto them during the trip. Both the kids and the dads enjoyed themselves. I felt delighted for the youngsters and had a twinge of regret for myself.

Seeing positive interactions can make you aware of what you missed. Establishing a baseline of what fathers *can* provide for their youngsters creates a fair standard of measure. Many of you blamed yourself for wanting too much as children, thinking, "I shouldn't have needed that from my dad." Viewing good fathering gives you permission to feel your own disappointment.

Give yourself the assignment of observing fathers and their children wherever you see them – stores, parks, movie lobbies. Some of the interactions may be loving and positive, some hurtful. Note how each father looks at his youngster. Consider how the child responds to dad. Be conscious of your own feelings as you watch these exchanges. You may be surprised at the intensity of your emotions.

One father-loss woman who took my seminar said that she didn't want to do this exercise. "It raises a lot of envy and anger in me," she explained. "My father saw me only once a year after the divorce when I was four. I've spent my whole life trying to cope with the hurt I felt when I was around other fathers and daughters."

DENIAL is not a river in Egypt.

This exercise is *meant* to break through denial to the deep feelings you have inside. Let yourself experience your emotions. You may notice any number of dads who do love and take care of their children. If you really allow this awareness to touch you, you probably *will* have a reaction.

Deepening Your Experience

At the end of many exercises, I give suggestions for added measures you can take to enhance and expand upon the work you've done. I encourage you to follow these recommendations to deepen your healing.

Write in your journal about the feelings that came up for you as you watched fathers and their children. Let your thoughts come straight from the heart.

Using your non-dominant hand, sketch one of the father/child interactions you witnessed that touched you. Or draw a memory of you and your dad together that stands out in your mind.

* All the drawings in this book are by father-wound workshop participants. They used their non-dominant hands to get in touch with intense childhood feelings about their dads.

EXERCISE 2.   HOW DAD AFFECTED YOU

This process gets you thinking about all aspects of your relationship with your father, nurturing as well as hurtful. You may also see the connections between your past struggles with your dad and the challenges in your present life.

To get a clear picture of your relationship with your father, draw a large circle, divide it into thirds, and label the sections: *Positives, Negatives,* and *Current Problems.*

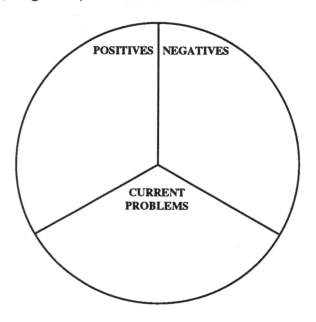

First, list your father's positive contributions to you and his good qualities. Second, note your dad's shortcomings. In what ways was his fathering inadequate? If he died young or you didn't know him well, write both the pluses and minuses of his not being around. Third, indicate the problem areas your life shows now. Give yourself five minutes at most. The idea is not to ponder deeply but to jot down quickly whatever comes to mind.

Just sit with these observations and let them percolate inside you. Their significance may be obvious to you right away, but you don't have to draw any immediate conclusions.

"This exercise made me see that my father gave me most of the material things I wanted, which were supposed to make up for his lack of closeness," one woman said after completing this exercise. "Maybe that was the only way he could express love. Now I'm trying to overcome needing to have someone spend money on me in order to feel valued."

INADEQUATE FATHERING

If you had a difficult relationship with your dad as a child, his treatment of you probably fits into one or more of the four broad categories of inadequate fathering: **absent, abusive, judgmental,** or **distant.** The way your dad dealt with you was a powerfully influential force that helped shape who you are. You can be sure that these imprints still impact you today. Unhealthy father/child interactions produce predictable outcomes. Locating yourself within these general patterns may enable you to be more objective about how your father affected you.

On reading the descriptions below, you may find that your father represents more than one type, since some of the boundaries overlap. Feel free to skip over depictions that obviously don't match your own experience – though reading them all may significantly broaden your understanding of the scope of father-loss.

After studying these profiles, you will have an opportunity to write about how your dad's traits fit into one or more of the various categories. By this means you can clarify his characteristics, your childhood response to them, and his effect on your adult life.

Absent Dads

An absent dad does not live with his child or is gone for significant periods of time. Prime examples are fathers who die prematurely or commit suicide, who divorce their wives and live apart from their youngsters, or who procreate a child without staying with the mother. A father in military service belongs in this group if he leaves the household for months-long stretches. Other instances are traveling dads who are away from home more than they are present, fathers who have been imprisoned for extensive terms, and those who simply desert their families.

What most father-absent children have in common is a debilitating fear of abandonment, the belief that everyone will leave them the way daddy did. They often feel ashamed and abnormal because they didn't have dads like other kids. In the self-centered world of children, it is easy and natural to harbor a deeply buried conviction that their absent fathers left *because of them.*

Deprivation of a dad sets up a profound hunger for fathering. Boys and girls long for someone to fill in what they are missing. The loss of father can elicit extreme feelings of dependence, which manifest themselves in several different ways. Youngsters may over-bond with their mothers, clinging to them for emotional support, while at the same time believing they must take care of mom because dad is gone. To compensate for a sense of helplessness early on, they often act inappropriately grown up. They may exhibit a pseudo-independence, yet lack a solid base of confidence and self-direction. As adults, children from absent-dad homes look for father substitutes in their romantic relationships. Having felt forsaken by their dads, they may obsessively pursue security by way of financial success. They may feel driven to seek validation through recognition and power.

Boys deprived of a dad lack a male role model, which leaves them with an underdeveloped sense of what it means to be a man. Often they have insufficient self-discipline and follow-through, as well as confusion about their career direction. They have lowered self-esteem and receive faulty preparation for subsequent male-female relationships.

Girls may not feel sure about their femininity, having lacked a father's regular interaction and endorsement. They have unrealistic expectations about what men are like. As adults, they may doubt their attractiveness and be uncertain about how to deal with sexuality. They yearn for intimacy with men but don't trust them. They tend to stay in unrewarding relationships longer than is good for them.

Abusive Dads

Abusive dads can be physically violent, rageaholic, sexually intrusive, or substance-addicted. Such fathers greatly damage their children. Because the assault is too much to comprehend, youngsters may react by cutting off from emotions, bodily sensations, and even memories. Yet feelings that are repressed and denied have to come out in some way. Physical illness, panic attacks, and addictions are among the ways people reveal their pain while concealing its actual origins.

Any abuse produces a profound sense of helplessness in a son or daughter. By repeatedly violating his child's boundaries, the father misuses his position of authority and trust. A youngster who feels no control over his or her own safety may accept abuse as a deserved punishment for some imagined personal failing, becoming fearful, withdrawn, and easily intimidated by others. Such a child may strive desperately to be the center of attention, out of a need for caring and approval. Or s/he might act out feelings of rage and hurt by coming into conflict with school or legal authorities.

These children often grow up to be victims or perpetrators of abuse themselves. Women who had abusive fathers often accept mistreatment in their adult lives. To compensate for their deep sense of powerlessness, men tend to reenact the abusive handling they received by raging at or being physically, sexually, or emotionally damaging to their own children.

Sexual abuse includes not only actual penetration but all the ways in which a father betrays his child's innocence and trust by inappropriate touches, looks, or suggestive talk and behavior. Because s/he wants to believe that dad is good and caring, the child takes on the blame, while continuing to idealize and protect him. Adults who had sexually abusive fathers tend toward the extremes of being either barely sexual or promiscuous. It is common for men and women who have been molested to be overweight. Layers of fat act as their protective buffer against those who frighten or could take advantage of them.

Addicted fathers model self-abusive behavior to their children. A dad's dependence on drugs or alcohol increases the likelihood of substance abuse by his son or daughter. These youngsters are prone to compulsive behaviors and addictions as ways to hide and relieve their pain.

Judgmental Dads

Judgmental dads are severely critical, controlling, and shaming. They have perfectionist expectations: whatever the child does, s/he cannot win dad's approval. Such fathers might communicate their preference for having had a child of a different sex. Sometimes they engage in harmful favoritism, continually criticizing one sibling, while another is treated as the special child.

Controlling dads injure their offspring emotionally by imposing too many limitations and rules. These men crush and invalidate their children's natural impulses by specifying too narrowly how to behave. Trying to please their fathers by living up to high standards, youngsters become anxious and exacting. They often suffer from despondency and can be unmercifully hard on themselves. They have low self-esteem and frequently experience profound shame and guilt.

Because their dads pressed them to be something they were not, these children usually have highly developed "false selves." They tend to hide their own desires and inner promptings, taking on characteristics and behaviors that conform to what pleases others. As adults, they often experience themselves as unformed, having skipped the normal phases of experimentation and self-expression in order to be what their fathers required. They may themselves become intolerant or dominant with others, repeating the paternal example.

Distant Dads

Children require a lot of attention and encouragement from their fathers. A distant dad injures by omission. He may be emotionally unavailable, a workaholic, or a step-father who never bonded with his children. He may watch TV incessantly, be chronically lost in depression, or obsess over sports or hobbies. He may be so invested in his own needs that he has little time or energy for his children. When he ignores or is too busy to deal with his child, a father conveys the message that his youngster's concerns are not as important to him as his own. When dad is in the house yet self-absorbed, a child is likely to conclude that father does not love him or her.

Neglect tends to leave these youngsters emotionally under-developed, lonely, and empty. The lack of interaction with their dads can influence them to substitute work for closeness or to make  do with minimal personal involvements. When they can't get their fathers to react to them, they may give up, suffering in silence. Or, feeling they have nothing to lose, they can misbehave to force their dad's interest. They engage in codependent behaviors that focus on the needs of others rather than their own internal pain. As adults, they long to be loved yet are wary of intimacy, believing that their needs can't or won't be met by a mate. They may feel they don't deserve to be loved.

Sometimes a father encourages false expectations, regularly making plans with his child that he does not carry out. Repeated broken promises can leave a son or daughter hurt, bitter, and suspicious. The youngster grows up repressed, mistrusting others, and lacking good communication skills.

A step-father is a special case – often a distant dad by definition. Starting as a stranger, he has to bridge a natural barrier against a male who arrives from outside to fill the paternal role. Sometimes, this new man turns out to be a great dad and friend. More frequently, however, the step-father and child do not develop a closeness that sufficiently overcomes the gulf between them. The relationship can range from a warm friendship at best to a neutral or chilly coexistence, including competition for mom's affection or outright hostility.

THE FATHER-WOUND

All children whose fathers were absent, abusive, judgmental, or distant carry deep pain inside. The father-wound causes scars that are visible in the child and persist in the adult. Youngsters learn to hide feelings, to isolate from others, or to act out hurts by misbehaving.

As adults, we father-wounded tend to under-achieve or over-work. Our dads' stinging criticism may compel us to succeed no matter what the personal cost. We could experience "father hunger," which is a deep yearning for paternal support. This need manifests itself as craving for attention from people in authority. We can make poor choices in mates. When we get into a relationship, we often find we aren't prepared to be intimate. Believing we don't merit love, we keep closeness from developing by enforcing emotional distance. *with friends as well*

Principal father-loss consequences include:

- mistrust
- envy
- bitterness or extreme anger
- addictions and obsessions
- a tendency to be self-critical and guilt-ridden
- excessive fear of rejection
- defensiveness
- fear of success
- a need to be in control

All in all, we father-loss people search for answers outside ourselves. We are out of touch with our feelings. We're more comfortable criticizing ourselves and others than we are being loving and accepting. We don't recognize and claim our own specialness. We live with an empty place inside that longs to be filled.

EXERCISE 3.   WHAT KIND OF FATHERING DID YOU HAVE?

The questions in this exercise intentionally probe into areas that are often difficult, complex, or distressing. The idea is to evoke deep and intense feelings and memories. I urge you to take the time and effort to answer them thoroughly. Your responses can give you invaluable self-awareness. After looking at your relationship with your dad from this perspective, you may understand, perhaps for the first time in your life, the correlation between your father's behavior toward you, your personality, and your problems.

Read questions "A" through "D" below. In your journal, write out answers to any of the questions which you feel apply to you and your dad. You may respond to one or more categories. Be specific, including as many details as you can recall. When describing feelings, use simple words like "hurt," "angry," "lonely," "sad," and "afraid" – to keep you in contact with your emotions rather than your thoughts.

If two or more men acted as your father, start with the one toward whom you feel the greatest visceral charge. If you feel you have significant issues with the others, re-do the exercise, focusing on each in turn.

A. Was your father absent?

- What were the conditions of his departure: death, suicide, divorce, military duty, extended travel, imprisonment, desertion?

- How old were you at the time?

- What feelings can you remember about his leaving?

- Did you ever think your father's absence was your fault?

- Did you talk about your dad being gone? How did your mother, siblings, grandparents, family friends, and others react to his absence?

- Did you exhibit an early independence? Describe what you did.

- Have you felt impeded in career development? In what way?

- Are you afraid that people you love will leave you?

- Can you identity any specific relationship problems that reflect your early experience with your father?

B. Was your father abusive?

- Recall some of the ways he was verbally, physically, or sexually damaging. How did you feel during and after these events?

- Do you have a sense that you've blocked out any memories or feelings from your childhood?

- If so, can you guess what kind of abuse you are repressing?

- What other family members were also mistreated?

- How did you feel about the way others did or did not protect you?
- Did your father exhibit addictive behaviors?
- Describe any problems you may have had yourself with overweight, substance abuse, or other compulsive behaviors.
- Have you gotten into trouble with any authorities?
- Do you let others abuse you now?
- Have you repeated the pattern of abuse with your children? How?
- How comfortable are you with your own sensuality and sexuality?
- How trusting and open are you in sexual intimacy?

C. Was your father judgmental?

- In what ways was he severe with you? Give examples of the comments he made or rules he enforced.
- How did he humiliate or stifle you? Recount three incidents in which he was hard on you.
- How did you feel before, during, and after these events?
- How did his judgments about you affect you later as an adult?

- Describe any mask you put on, or false self you developed, in order to please your dad.

- What kinds of self-criticism do you engage in?

- What other effects can you identify in your adult life which derive from your father's treatment of you during childhood?

D. Was your father distant?

- Describe in detail how he separated himself from you.

- Recall three specific times when he wasn't available to you. How did you feel inside?

But Daddy you are standing right here. How come you won't talk to me?

Not now, dear. I'm busy. Don't bother me.

But you're not doing anything right now. Can I just be by you, Dad?

I need to be left alone. Give me time, Candi. Go on.

Okay Dad. I'll leave you alone. I won't bug you any more.

- What did you do to get your father's attention? Were your actions successful? Do you continue the same behavior now with loved ones and authority figures?

- If you had a step-father, how old were you when he came on the scene? Examine the nature and trace the history of the relationship you had with him.

Deepening Your Experience

Using your non-dominant hand, draw a family portrait. Stop and do your sketch before you continue reading.

Now that you have created your picture, ask yourself the following questions to understand your dad's position in the family and the tone he set.

- Is your father physically touching any other member of the family?

- Does he seem to be emotionally connected to the others? For example, is he looking at anyone?

- Do you, he, and other family members lack any features: hands (signifying power), feet (grounding), eyes (ability to see), ears (ability to hear), or mouth (ability to speak)?

Make a collage illustrating what it was like to grow up with your father, or if he was absent, without his presence. Hang this montage in a prominent place so you can frequently recall your father's influence on you.

To make your collage, get a large piece of poster board or cardboard to which you can attach images, words, and even small objects in any arrangement that pleases you. You can use old photographs, illustrations and headlines from magazines, newspaper clippings, postcards, greeting cards – any item that seems significant or emotionally relevant. Affixing articles that hold meaning for you, such as medals, ribbons, or pressed flowers, can give your art piece texture and dimension.

PROBING THE PAST

Once you've started to understand how your insufficient fathering has affected your life, you're ready to dig deeper into your past. Often what seems forgotten is merely repressed. Just *wanting* to reclaim your history is a good starting place. You can be certain that re-examining as an adult your childhood reactions to your father will eventually enable you to see him differently. The more open you are to letting this information emerge, whether pleasant or painful, the more easily the memories and feelings will come back to you.

You may believe you feel nothing now. Indeed, emotions are like a panel of lights on a single switch. You can't turn off only the ones that hurt. When you numb yourself to pain, *all* your responses reduce in sensitivity. Once you allow your feelings to come to life, you can experience your joy as well as your anguish. By re-establishing contact with suppressed parts of your past, you gain a new connection to the present.

EXERCISE 4. RECLAIM YOUR PAST

Make a point of beginning to reconstruct the past by talking with members of your family: your mother, grandparents, brothers and sisters, aunts and uncles – even your father himself. As they reminisce, you'll learn and remember more about you and your dad. You may hear conflicting information from different family members. Keep in mind that everyone has his or her own version of reality. Each viewpoint reveals as much about the person as about what happened.

Allow yourself to experience whatever emotions come up for you. Facts are important, but even more significant are the feelings attached to events. As you increase your awareness of the origins of your character traits and attitudes, you are actually reclaiming more of yourself.

For some, this may require extensive research. It could involve writing letters to family and friends in distant places or even a trip across the country. It is worth the effort it takes to get more in touch with your roots.

Another doorway to your father memories is drawing the floor plan of the house or apartment where you grew up. In which room did dad spend most of his time? Where did you?

Where was his chair? How did it smell? If you had multiple homes, choose the one that was most significant to you. Let yourself remember all the details of living with your father – and recall how you felt about him and yourself.

A client's comment reveals just how helpful reconnecting with familiar places and sensations can be in unlocking memories: "I looked up school records and the addresses of former residences, then went to the old locations and walked around. This was very valuable for unblocking repressed material. I also listened to old TV series, ads and commercials, songs, and music from my early years. I even recalled key smells! It's incredible what can break open bottled-up memories."

Deepening Your Experience

As you collect information, jot down in your journal some of the anecdotes you haven't heard before. Putting all these stories in order to create a short biography on your dad might give you a surprising degree of insight into his life.

While focusing on your early childhood, don't overlook the pivotal period of your adolescence. In your journal, be sure to include recollections of your teenage experiences with your father.

Getting in touch with your feelings is essential to working through your father issues. At first, as you do the exercises, the emotions that come up may baffle or overwhelm you. Like a jack-in-the-box, releasing what you have long held down will bring a lot back forcefully. Just accept these intense feelings as a normal part of the process. If you find yourself upset or frightened, don't be worried. Reach out to others when you need reassurance. Share your experiences with someone who feels safe. You may want to contact a professional counselor to help you understand your responses to these memories.

If nothing seems to be happening for you, that's okay too. Be patient. Give yourself the space to react and progress at a pace that feels right. Everyone unfolds in his or her own way.

EXERCISE 5. WHAT DID YOU MISS?

The purpose of this exercise is to visualize a nurturing experience between you and your father. What you imagine need not be based on an actual memory. Visualization is like a waking dream in which you ask your imagination to produce a scene you can enter. The vividness of such a scenario can help you bring up previously unacknowledged feelings or facts. Creating pictures in your mind's eye provides clues to what's going on at deep, often hard-to-reach levels of your being.

Some of you may find it difficult to imagine a positive interaction with your dad. Don't be discouraged if nothing emerges at first. Just relax and ask your inner self to come up with relevant images.

Read the following guided visualization into a tape recorder. Go very slowly, adding pauses where appropriate. Give your voice a gentle, soothing intonation. Play the tape back in a quiet place. If you don't wish to use a tape machine, just read the meditation aloud to yourself. Let your imagination create a special vision of you and your dad. You may want to dim the lights and play soft music to encourage a free flow of ideas.

Guided Visualization: (Begin recording.)

Picture yourself as a child. How old are you? Are you an infant, an adolescent, or somewhere in between? If an image does not immediately come to mind, allow yourself to walk back in time through your childhood years. What age attracts you the most? Any period that you choose is the right one for you. Can you see what you're wearing? Where are you? In a house? Outside? Are you alone? With friends or family? Allow yourself to fill in as much detail as possible. What do you see as you look around? Let colors, sounds, and smells fill your scene.

Now, see your dad coming into the setting where you are as a youngster. Can you remember a warmhearted time you shared with him? Was there an incident when you two felt especially close? If it is too difficult or scary for you to bring in your dad, use another father figure, perhaps a friend's dad or an ideal father that you make up. It doesn't matter who the dad is. A deep inner part of you needs an image of a father who is kind, open, and encouraging.

If you can recall a specific tender occasion with your dad, let that experience play out as though you are watching a movie. Envision the beginning, middle, and end of the event you participate in together. Fill the scene with as many details as you can. If a specific happening with your dad does not come to mind, let yourself create an encounter that you would have wanted to have with him.

Observe carefully your father's disposition and actions. How near is he to you? Does he touch or hold you? What are his words? What is the look on his face? What are his eyes saying? As a child, how do you feel being with your dad in this touching moment?

(End recording.)

Remembering this time with your dad may leave you very happy. It could also move you to tears. Let yourself enjoy and savor this experience. Take it inside you and know that this memory is now part of you to draw on whenever you wish. Once you have completed the visualization, write down in your journal what you saw yourself doing with your father.

Whatever you envisioned can give you a clue to what you most wanted from your father. For example, one woman saw herself at the age of five years old with her dad in a vegetable garden, digging in the rich soil and planting seeds. What she most desired was to share quality time with her father. This interaction could have enriched the roots of her being and helped germinate grounded, lively, and healthy relationships with other men.

Other workshop participants reported the following experiences.

"I see my dad and myself fishing at a lake we went to together one time when I was around nine or ten years old. I felt special, loved, and important because he wanted to take me with him."

"I picture myself at about five years old, sitting outside on the milk box. It's summer, bright, sunny, and warm. My father comes along and picks me up and just holds me gently for a long while. He kisses me a few times, and we talk about what a pretty day it is, and he tells me how much he loves me."

"I picture myself at my Sweet Sixteen party. My father is so proud. He has tears in his eyes. All he keeps saying is, 'I'm so proud of how you've turned out to be such a beautiful young woman.'"

As one student pointed out: "This was good for me, because it made me realize I can create my own father image within myself. I can trust him to stay, because he is inside of *me.*"

Resist any temptation to skip over this exercise. Visualization may be hard for some. For others, thinking of a pleasant experience with your father will spark off painful reminders of what you missed. Still others will have a lot of trouble recreating a tender moment with their dads. Give yourself a chance to have a positive memory of your father.

Deepening Your Experience

Draw the scene you imagined where you and your dad shared a delightful activity or a special moment together.

CYNDEE & DADDY READING & PLAYING TOGETHER

EXERCISE 6. LOCATE DAD WITHIN YOU

This exercise sharpens your intuitive perception of how you are relating to your father now. Creative imaging can be an effective technique for experiencing his actual place in your life.

Once you read the following instructions through, you can use lowered lights and soothing background music to help induce receptivity. Sit comfortably and close your eyes. Breathe deeply, letting yourself get very quiet.

After several minutes, when you have stilled yourself as much as possible, feel where your father is *in your body*. Open yourself to the experience of locating where you physically hold your dad inside you.

- **Is he in the center or attached to the bottom of your heart?**

- **Is he in the pit of your stomach, caught in your throat, or hiding at the back of your head?**

- **What does he feel like?**

Just stay with that spot. Now imagine that the part of your body where you have discovered your dad can communicate.

- **Does this site have a message for you?**

- **What does it say? Let the phrases come quickly. Don't intellectualize about them. If you draw a blank, give the emptiness a voice.**

- **If you hardly knew your dad, where in your body do you sense his absence? Let whatever feeling is associated with that place speak.**

"My dad is in my throat," one woman indicated. "I've never been able to tell him how sad he made me and my mother. It's too late now. He's too old. He wouldn't be able to handle or understand it. He's been lost without my mother since she died. It would be cruel to tell him. Still, I feel I have to help him get on with his life."

This person may choose not to tell her father how she feels, yet she can express her emotion to others. Locating her father in her body gave her an opportunity to get in touch with suppressed conflicts that were important for her to rediscover.

Here are reports from others who tried this exercise:

"My father was in my knees. He always had bad knees, and I have a slight problem in my left knee, although I never damaged it to my memory. He also cuts me down at my knees – I can't run from him, and I can't walk on my own. I feel lame, because of my father in my knees."

"He's in the pit of my stomach and in my jaws that I keep clenched tight. I'm afraid that I could let out secrets about my dad to other people who might not understand me."

"My dad was on my back. Growing up and as an adult, I felt such concern for him. I believed I had to take care of myself and him, because he seemed so lost most of the time."

Congratulations for making it through the first section! Beginning a challenging trek is the hardest part. This workbook provides you with a carefully thought-out and structured healing plan. As a father-loss veteran, I have experienced this process from both sides, being in recovery myself and having led thousands of people through it. I know these exercises will continue to work for you, if you stick with the program.

The next segment also requires demanding emotional struggle, but making the effort and putting up with any discomfort will pay off. You will feel liberated as you release your pain and fears and put your past behind you. This healing readies you to take positive action toward improving your present life.

If you're not getting in touch with your feelings yet, give yourself time. The psyche responds best to frequent invitations to feel, to let go, to love. Keep doing the exercises and be patient. You may get into this method only little by little. Be ready to fan any spark of emotion or interest that comes. If you skipped over some of the exercises, or believe you have more work to do on any particular one, feel free to go back and give yourself another chance. Each provides an important building-block in remaking yourself.

Remember not to rush through the material. You need to digest what you experience in order to process your feelings. Doing one exercise every couple of days is fast enough. Even if you are just reading without doing the exercises, I recommend you go slowly. Trying to grasp the whole in a few prolonged sessions may leave you overwhelmed, because there is a lot of information to respond to and absorb.

I understand how natural it is to resist doing this work. One woman said honestly, "At first I didn't want to do this, but once I got going, it brought up a lot of feelings that I usually put aside or haven't dealt with yet." If you experience a great deal of unwillingness, proceed slowly and gently, preferably working with a group, friend, or counselor.

Recovery work is like going swimming in the ocean, which certainly can be scary. You are immersed in an immense force over which you lack total control. You could get hurt, yet there are benefits to be gained – health, exhilaration, and a sense of accomplishment. When you emerge from the water, you feel strengthened and refreshed. However you accomplish it, do yourself the favor of diving in, despite your fears. You can achieve a new level of freedom.

So far, you have watched fathers and children interacting, looked at your own father's positive and negative qualities, and gotten in touch with the effects of your father-wound. You've discovered ways to claim more of your past, uncovered what you have yearned for in a father, and found out where your dad symbolically lives in you. Now it's time to move into the sorrow that is in your heart and learn how to release it.

SECTION TWO

MOURNING AND LETTING GO OF YOUR PAIN

Once we acknowledge what we didn't get from our fathers, the next step is to mourn our loss. While realization is mainly an intellectual process, grieving is primarily emotional. Now we want to allow ourselves to deal with our anger and sadness connected with our fathers. Most of us block the expression of such unpleasant buried feelings, so it isn't easy to get in touch with our pain. Yet *feeling* the sadness is the key to healing.

Feeling sad is the normal and natural response to loss. But how many of us as children were encouraged to show our sorrow? When a father dies or leaves, children are not usually supported in grieving. Adults don't know how to deal with grief either, so both they and the youngsters suffer in silence. The conventional wisdom of previous generations has dictated that if the children focus on daily routines and don't talk much about their father, they will recover from their loss more quickly. Instead, such suppression simply buries the pain, leaving it unresolved.

> **Expressing sadness is healing.**

We need to put sounds to the painful empty places within us. We can allow ourselves to weep, moan, sniffle, break down – whatever it takes to get those stuck feelings out. Anger and sadness held inside indefinitely turn into depression, bitterness, and hostility. Crying is a cleansing process to our eyes, minds, and hearts. It is like washing a window to let in the sunshine. Through clean glass, we can see how much is happening in the world outside.

To mourn well is to live well. Loss in life is inevitable. There is a natural cycle to grieving. Rather than avoiding the pain of deprivation, staying with it over time makes it possible to let it go. This release creates the space in our lives to bring in new satisfaction and joy. Even after all these years, expressing old feelings will free up the energy we have been using to keep them tucked away.

GETTING IN TOUCH WITH THE HURT

In order to mourn the pain you experienced regarding your father, consider your relationship with him from your point of view as a child. This is your starting place, because it is the *child* within you that was injured or deprived. You can look both at what you lacked as a result of your father not being available to you and at any ways he actively hurt you.

Even if the reasons you suffered were out of your father's control, such as death or sickness, you can still acknowledge the pain you felt as a youngster. If your family didn't encourage you to express your emotions at the time, then those reactions stayed locked inside.

Some people fear getting stuck in the grieving process. They think they'll be sad forever. Yet if they try to avoid the pain, it controls them. They live in a state of suffering, not feeling the loss acutely, but not moving beyond it either.

> **The only way out is through.**

Unresolved feelings don't age well. They curdle into resentment and negativity. It's vital to release these old unexpressed attitudes. The exercises in this section are designed to show you how to let go of your hurt and anger. By clearing away your previous pain, you prepare for personal reconstruction, just as workmen rid a homesite of debris before they build a new house.

Take into account that you were only a child, while your father was an adult. Whatever problems he may have had, his role was to protect, guide, and take care of you. Often a youngster feels guilty when dad is upset or depressed for reasons that have nothing to do with the child's conduct. Even an abused child can assume the blame for dad's misbehavior. It is entirely appropriate for you to relinquish any youthful self-reproach that you're carrying regarding your father. Responsibility for his actions belongs to him.

When you become aware of your past, you can free yourself from it, releasing the hold your early experiences and beliefs have on you in the present. Doing so is like bringing memories and feelings up from a dank and scary cellar into the light.

EXERCISE 7. DISAPPOINTMENT WITH DAD

Before you can express your anger and pain, you have to let yourself remember what wounded you. You may be aware that your father failed you yet deny the degree of your injury. This exercise can help get you in touch with the anguish and disappointment you felt regarding your dad.

Begin by thinking of all the actions you believe your dad neglected to do for you or did badly. The following questions will help you remember and reflect upon incidents from the past. *Take your time* as you read through them. Pay attention to whether your body reveals any emotional reactions. Trust whatever comes up for you. Each person's perception of reality is what s/he needs to acknowledge and process, regardless of what you may have heard from other family members.

- How much time did your father spend with you?

- How much of himself did he express to you, and how well did he listen to you?

- Did he keep his agreements with you?

- What judgments about you did your father spell out?

- How did you feel in response to specific actions or inaction on his part?

After you have considered these questions, review the following exercise until you understand all its parts. Then record the guided meditation out loud onto a cassette, speaking slowly in a gentle voice. This will help to put you in a receptive frame of mind for contacting your childhood feelings. If the phrases seem right for you, take them in and permit them to touch you. If they do not seem appropriate to you, just let them go by.

Guided Meditation:

Dad, you meant so much to me. I needed a daddy to cherish and protect me. I was young and vulnerable. I needed you. I wanted you to love me, and I wanted to love you. I felt so alone without your love. There is an emptiness inside me because I feel you weren't there for me.

I'm sure there were reasons things happened the way they did, but I was a child and didn't realize the causes. I just know I needed you to understand me, to comfort me, to let me know you cared. I wanted you to have confidence in me, so I could believe in myself. I figured everything was my fault somehow. I thought, "If only I could be different, if only I could be better."

Sometimes now I'm angry at you, but mostly I'm just sad for all that we missed. There were so many times I hurt because of you. Where were you when I needed you, Dad?

Close your eyes, breathe deeply, and relax. Play the recording back. Then open your eyes. While still in this quiet state, write down specific incidents when you felt your father let you down. Start with the words: *"Dad, when you..."* Fill in a personal experience. Then add your response to his action, using the phrase, *"I felt..."* For example, "Dad, when you didn't believe me the time my scout leader blamed me unfairly, I felt abandoned." Or, "Dad, when you didn't attend my high school graduation, I felt angry and sad."

Often people have difficulty remembering particular events. Just be patient with yourself, and something will come. Write out now as many completions as you can to the sentence, *"Dad, when you..., I felt..."* Or you may choose to simply speak your memories into the tape recorder. As other recollections surface, you can keep listing more disappointments.

Once again, I recommend that you use simple words to capture your feelings, such as "sad," "hurt," "angry," "afraid," "lonely," and "ashamed." The little child in you can relate to these basic emotions. You may have more than one feeling at a time. You needn't justify your emotions by stating why you felt the way you did. Feelings just are. Explaining them takes you away from your heart into your head.

As you become more aware of your sentiments about your dad, you may find yourself feeling guilty. You may believe you are betraying your father. The very act of thinking negative thoughts about him could distress you. Rather than make yourself wrong, learn to view your own needs as primary. This shift to a concern for the importance of your feelings can be a major step in your growth process.

Deepening Your Experience

In your journal, address these questions:

- How much grieving have I actually done regarding my dad?

- When did I do it, and under what circumstances?

- Did I have support?

- What was the result?

- What has been my pattern for dealing with sadness in my life?

- Does the way I have dealt with sadness correlate to how I have handled my feelings about my father?

With your non-dominant hand, portray in a picture one childhood situation when you felt sad because of your dad. Stop now and draw before you read on.

After you finish the drawing, ask some questions about the meaning of your figures. Are you and your father looking at each other? Are you interacting or acting separately? What is the feeling between you and him?

INVENTORY HIS OFFENSES

Through the sins of *omission* that you've just reviewed, your dad let you down. In sins of *commission*, he took actions that directly hurt you. Most of you have been carrying around such father-wounds for a very long while. You may have harbored blame toward your father, saying to yourself, "How could my dad have done that to me? That was unforgivable!"

> **Unexpressed pain doesn't go away, because it gets buried ALIVE.**

It is important to clearly identify the wrongs for which you still feel your father is accountable. Invoke your righteous anger regarding his mistreatment. Releasing feelings is a difficult process. It is best done in stages, the first of which is to indicate precisely what you hold against your dad. Until you've uncovered and aired your complaints, there is little chance you'll let them go.

EXERCISE 8.   ASSESS YOUR GRIEVANCES

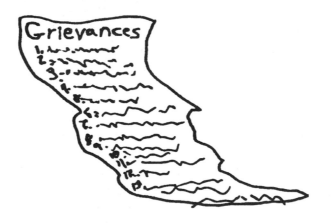

Begin by taking stock of what you resent about your father's behavior. Write out completions to this statement, *"One thing I don't forgive my father for is . . ."*   Keep finishing this sentence until you have exhausted your entire inventory of grievances toward him.

Important note: put this list aside. You will work with it again in a later exercise on forgiveness.

This is your time to be totally honest about your hurts. Don't minimize your true feelings in an attempt to protect your dad. Consider carefully what you're not ready to forgive. If you have a hard time coming up with something to write, sit still for ten minutes. Then put down whatever comes into your mind.

You should not forgive before you're ready. You may have been taught that forgiveness simply involves a conscious act of will – all you need do is make the decision. Not so. Forgiving is a process. Unless your whole being is willing to pardon, sooner or later you will find yourself upset and resentful again. Cutting short your expression of hurt and anger is counterproductive.

ACKNOWLEDGING ANGER

Are you afraid of your anger, denying that it even exists? Or are you sometimes frightened by the intensity of your fury? Constructive anger provides you with energy to stand up for yourself and persevere toward your goals. Manifesting your irritation in a direct, clear manner helps you claim your power and set limits that protect you from abuse. If you don't release your wrath, you can collapse into depression.

Why do father-wounded adults have such difficulty expressing their anger? For many, showing temper was not acceptable in their family when they were growing up. Despite their best efforts to maintain control, they still may find themselves in the middle of unwanted temper tantrums. Some were frightened by a father's destructive fury. Anger can be hurtful, even lethal. Many such fearful children vowed they would not vent their own rage on others. Now they may hide their legitimate vexation in suffering. Feeling like victims, they can easily break down into tears.

> **A whine is anger coming out of a little hole.**

"I'm stuck in sadness," one workshop member confided. "I cannot give myself permission to just be angry with my father and get over it. I'm terrified of my anger. It's considered a dangerous thing in my family, so I suppress it."

You have a right to your rage. To express it is to validate it. To even consider voicing your wrath, you will have to face your darker side, which is as powerful and beneficial as your light. One can't exist without the other. The idea is to let go of your negativity instead of being stuck in it. You get relief from the pressure of holding it inside you.

EXERCISE 9. EXPRESS YOUR ANGER CONSTRUCTIVELY

You may have blocks to connecting with your anger. You probably didn't have good models for airing it appropriately. You may tend to minimize or laugh off what irritates you. If you don't get to the root of what bothers you, incidents that may appear insignificant can easily trigger your hostility.

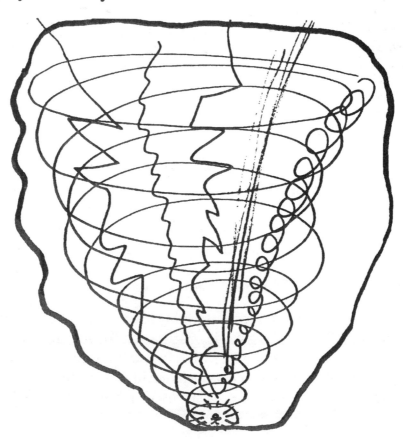

If you have suppressed your anger toward your father, you may not be aware that your body is storing it in the form of a headache, clenched jaw, knotted stomach, taut shoulders, or over-all muscle tightness.

The following exercises are designed to help release any anger trapped in your body. At first, you may feel inhibited, but after doing them, you will feel glad to have a way to effectively reduce the tensions and frustrations of daily living. You may have to do these movements many times to feel purged of your deep-seated fury.

This exercise sequence may require more planning than some of the others. Forewarn family members about the noise, or practice only when you are in the house alone. Shut your windows. Play loud music. After all, you wouldn't want neighbors rushing in to save you from imagined intruders, when you're just letting off steam! In doing this clearing, you may find yourself getting deeply into your rage or taking pleasure in bellowing and ranting. Both responses are good.

Focus on your anger toward your dad. If you haven't allowed yourself to feel enraged at him, you may have to pretend. *Act as if* you feel upset, until the feeling catches up to the behavior. It can be fun to do these exercises with a friend or group. Powerful, throbbing music can prime you to let out your anger.

---

1. Breathe and groan.

Stand with your feet flat, a shoulder's-width apart. Breathe deeply from your abdomen. As you exhale, let sounds come out, like "Ah-h-h-h." Breathe through your mouth, keeping your chin loose and relaxed, making deep groans, moans, and sighs that release the pain and tension from inside. At first, this may seem strange, but stay with it. Your body will feel much lighter when it's allowed to express itself in free-form noises.

2. Make elbow and arm circles.

Still standing with your feet comfortably apart, tuck each hand up into its shoulder pit. Start making circles with your elbows, alternating one arm and then the other. Do a half dozen *slow* rotations, feeling the energy opening up in your torso, shoulders, and back. Then fully extend your arms to make large circles, reaching out with your fingers stretched. Keep breathing with your mouth open and chin relaxed, while continuing to groan. Now repeat the process, making the elbow and then arm circles in the opposite direction.

3. Do head circles.

Make slow circles with your head hanging limp, keeping your back straight and motionless. You may hear a lot of cracking and popping. That's tension breaking up. Keep breathing and groaning as you continue the head motions. You should feel more relaxed and in touch with your body by this point.

4. *"Get off my back!"*

Visualize all the hurt and suffering that comes from your father as settling on your back and shoulders like a heavy load. Taking care not to strain your muscles, forcibly jerk one elbow at a time behind you at shoulder level and shout, *"Get off my back! Get off my back! Get off my back!"* Do this a dozen times or until you're spent and feel unburdened.

5. *"Don't hurt me!"*

Forcibly push one arm out in front of you with your hand up, like a policeman stopping traffic. Hold for just a moment, pull back, then extend your other hand. Keep alternating arms as you speak out loudly, *"Don't hurt me! Stop! That's enough! No more!"* If other short, direct phrases have more meaning to you, use whatever ones come to mind that fit your situation. Repeat these declarations at least a dozen times, allowing more and more power into your voice.

6. Have a temper tantrum.

There are two ways to have a tantrum. Whichever you choose, this is a valuable device to release your pent-up anger. You can sit in a chair, stamp your feet, vigorously shake your fists up and down in front of you, and yell out, *"No! No! No! No! No! No! I won't! I won't! I won't!"* Or, lie on your back on a bed and kick your legs and pound with your arms, screaming the same words. Do either of these until you're exhausted.

7. Rip pages from an old telephone book.

Take a phone directory you are no longer using. Sit on the floor. Tear out one leaf at a time. As you crumple the page into a ball and throw it across the room, blurt out an angry thought about your father. With each sheet, say one phrase loudly. For example, you might shout, *"Dad, don't touch me!," "You hurt me,"* or *"You never took care of us."* You might try expressions such as, *"Dad, I hate you," "You made everything my fault,"* or *"I'd like to punch you in the gut."* Don't worry about the intensity or propriety of what you say. This is just between you and the phone book. Other variations are to shred the pages into little pieces or twist a couple of them into a tight wad as you talk. Keep this up until you feel finished. For most people it takes ten to thirty pages, but don't be reluctant to use even more!

One class member did this exercise before going to bed. After she got out all her anger, she went right to sleep, exhausted. In the morning she awoke to a room filled with yellow balls of paper. Out of curiosity, she counted them: there were sixty-eight.

In a safe place, such as an outdoor fire ring or your fireplace, you may enjoy burning the crumpled pages. You can watch your feelings go up in smoke, letting the fire purify and release your rage. You will feel satisfaction in seeing the flames your anger has produced reduce into nothing but ashes that blow away easily in the wind.

8. Pound a pillow.

Put a big pillow on a bed, chair, or the floor. Kneel in front of it. Use your fists and forearms to repeatedly pound the pillow, shouting at the same time, *"How could you do that to me? I'm angry. I'm mad."* When you swing down, be careful that you lower your head along with your arms, so that you don't strain your back. Continue hitting rigorously until you have no more energy left, which usually takes less than ten minutes.

9. Use your ingenuity.

You can come up with other active movements that will help you let go of your anger. A friend of mine releases her outrage with paints and a large canvas, using bold brush strokes of intense color. You might exorcize your wrath by dancing free-spirited to rousing music. How about keeping a punching bag in the kitchen? For greater release, add angry words that express what you feel. You could scream into a thick towel. Or roll up your automobile windows and use the vehicle as a sound insulation chamber. It's amazing how loudly you can shout in your car without being heard. Be inventive, even outrageous, as long as it stays safe for you and everyone else.

You might be confused or even startled to find yourself coming out with so much rage. You may have doubted that you had such intense ire inside you. It was there all along, but you're just now giving yourself permission to feel it.

When you have discharged your anger to the point where you feel drained, then it is time to soothe yourself. You can visualize a healing white light surrounding your body. You may want to rest. Do any activity that is calming or nurturing for you, such as indulging in a long warm bath, sipping a cup of hot tea, playing soft music, or taking a walk.

Deepening Your Experience

Tell your journal how you customarily deal with angry feelings when they arise. Is that how your father expressed rage or how you responded to him?

Symbolize in a drawing your anger about your dad. Some people use heavy black or red crayon marks to express the intensity of their experience. Others depict objects like pressure cookers or powerful forces of nature, like torrents of water, thunderbolts, or erupting volcanoes.

PUTTING FEELINGS INTO WORDS

You can continue clearing out old emotions through an exercise that gives you an opportunity to imagine yourself speaking your deepest feelings to your father. This can help you express reactions that you may never have articulated to him. To prepare for what you might tell your dad, listen to what one forty-year-old woman had to say to her father when she did this process.

Dear Dad,

I love you. Do you realize I have never, ever heard those words from you, nor was I able to say them to you? How strange! Why, Dad, why couldn't you let me see something, anything that made me feel you cared about me? You showed no emotion when I was little. Do you know how lonely that was for me? I didn't realize it then. How could I? I thought that was just the way things were.

The funny thing is, Dad, that after I got married, I realized my relationship with Bob was just like the one I had with you. Bob was weak, Dad, like you. He would say he loved me, but there was no feeling. It took me 40 years to know and learn what love is, and what it isn't. If only you could have loved me, Dad, I would not have married the first man who came along and noticed me. I think I would have married anyone who asked me - any man who told me nice things. Oh, I'm so angry, Dad! Just maybe if you did the things you were supposed to do, I wouldn't be hurting now.

I'm hurting, and so are my children. Because you didn't love me, I accepted Bob's unemotional ways toward our children. Now they say they don't feel loved.

I'm afraid, Dad, that I won't be able to come out of this and be all that I can for myself and my children. I'm afraid you might die soon, and I won't be able to say "I love you," and I'll regret it all my life.

I love you, Dad. Please know that.

> *Your daughter,*
> *Kelly*

Your hurt little child needs to be able to say whatever s/he feels toward your father. In this case, the writer seems to be blaming her dad for her own poor choices. Eventually she will have to accept responsibility for what she has created in her life. Here, however, we are concentrating on the expression of emotions, not on identifying accountability.

EXERCISE 10. HONESTY WITH FATHER

This is your opportunity to tell your father (or your step-father) everything you've ever wanted to tell him. Perhaps in the past you tried to get him to admit the mistakes he made with you or to show you more of his love. Now, through role-playing, you can focus on *your* thoughts and feelings rather than on his response to you. Because you're not actually talking to him, you don't have to worry about hurting him or how he would answer back.

Settle into a quiet place and read through the following thoughts, allowing past interactions with your dad to surface. If you could say anything to your father, what would you want to bring up? These questions may trigger some ideas:

- Are there resentments you've held back from your dad?

- Do you have anger you haven't expressed yet?

- Do you want to tell him about how frightened, lonely, or empty you felt as his child?

- Do you have questions you've held back from asking him?

- Do you want to tell him what you needed and wanted from him when you were growing up?

- Do you wish he could know about the times you were hurt and sad?

- Do you have regrets you want to share with him?

- Do you feel you love him, but you haven't put your affection into words?

If your father was absent or you didn't know your father well enough to have a relationship with him, tell him your thoughts and feelings about growing up without him there.

- What was it like to be different from other children who did have fathers or felt close to their fathers?

- What did his absence mean to you as a child, a teen, and as you became an adult?

- Did you long for your father?

- Were you angry he wasn't there?

Get your tape recorder ready. Read through the following instructions. Then begin by closing your eyes. Become aware of your breath. Shallow breathing indicates that you're afraid to fully feel what you are experiencing. The key to openness is deep breathing. Inhale deeply for several minutes. Relax and let yourself get centered.

Imagine your father sitting across from you. Let yourself really see him. How old is he? Any age you picture him is all right. What is the look on his face? You can visualize him near you or at a bit of a distance. The basic ground rule is that he can

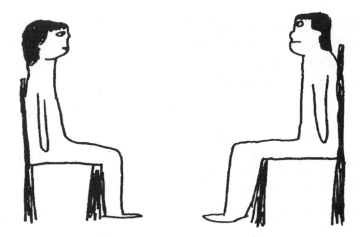

only listen and not respond in any way. This is *your* chance to speak to him about the emotions you have had toward him throughout your life. The more detailed you can be about specific incidents and your reactions to them, the better.

Turn on your tape recorder. Out loud, tell your dad all the feelings that you never told him or need to tell him again. Voice everything that is in your heart. Experience your emotions as deeply as you can. Let tears and pain flow out of you. Healing comes from putting words to feelings as they move through you. Explain to your father who you really are and what you feel. Take risks and be vulnerable.

If you're doing this exercise in a group, members should form into pairs. Sit across from your partner and get positioned so you can comfortably hold hands. It is important to physically connect with the other person during this emotional risk-taking. Close your eyes, pretend you're sitting facing your father, and speak as if to your dad. If you run out of words to say to him, just wait. When you think of something else you want to say, begin again. Each person takes a reasonable amount of time to say what is important. In seminars, I allocate about ten minutes per person.

The individual who is not talking witnesses the partner's words and feelings silently. Under no circumstances should the listener make comments, offer suggestions, or give comfort. S/he just provides support for the speaker. Each person must face dad alone, on his or her own terms.

One workshop participant commented. "What's good about *pretending* my dad was there is that I got a chance to say exactly what I wanted. In real life, I watch for his reaction. This way, I said it for me, not for him."

Another person shared, "When I first read through this exercise, I couldn't imagine myself doing it. 'No way,' I said to myself. Then when it came time in class, I just did it – and got so much out of it."

FINDING A KEY TO YOUR EMOTIONS

Getting in touch with your feelings is a fundamental step toward personal change. Now that you are beginning to expose emotions you may not have realized you had, it's time to take a closer look at how they work. They reveal themselves through your body. Your heart can ache when you're sad. Your eyes will feel pressured when you want to cry but don't. To remain unaffected by the hurt and anger contained in your body, you have to sever your most basic connection with yourself.

To contact your feelings more fully, you can focus on the physical sensations you're experiencing. For example, whenever your throat starts tightening under stress, you probably are cutting off words you want to say and sounds you need to make. I can remember pain in my throat so intense at times it seemed as though knives were piercing either side of my larynx, a sure signal I wasn't verbalizing something important.

As you go through your day, and especially when you do the exercises in this book, look for occasions when your eyes feel tight, your heart speeds up, your throat catches, or your stomach clenches into a knot. Once you associate each sensation with particular feelings, you will start to better understand where in your body you are blocking their expression. Many people fear strong emotions, until they learn that it is safe and beneficial to experience them.

EXERCISE 11.   "DADDY, DADDY, DADDY"

The word that you call your father is emotionally laden. Vocalizing this name lets you experience a broad range of feelings toward him. This exercise may seem deceptively simple. Don't pass over it.

In a quiet place by yourself, practice expressing your emotions. By saying *"Daddy... Daddy... Daddy..."* in a variety of ways, you can experiment with sensations you may normally not let yourself feel. If *"Daddy"* doesn't fit with what you called your father, use whatever word is right for you: *"Dad," "Papa," "Father..."*

Speak *out loud.* Use the volume appropriate to the following sentiments, from a whisper to a shout. First, repeat "Dad" six or more times with ANGER in your voice. Next, address him a half-dozen times sounding HURT. Then use FEAR. Follow with LONGING. Then indicate FORGIVENESS. Finally, speak with LOVE. Notice what you are feeling and how your body reacts as you communicate each emotion.

One woman said about this exercise, "When I whispered 'Daddy' with longing in my voice, my chest trembled and my eyes tensed. I realized how, long ago, I quit asking anything of him. Consequently, when I became an adult, I didn't know how to ask men for what I wanted. I simply did things for myself. This time, I was able to feel my longing instead of the numbness I usually feel."

LAYERS OF FEELING

Feelings tend to unfold in layers, like an archaeological dig revealing era after era, each buried under the other. Usually *anger* is closest to the surface. Releasing that anger reveals the *hurt* and *sadness* below it. Experiencing the hurt uncovers the *fear* beneath the anger. Acknowledging the fear exposes our *unmet needs*. Dealing with those needs frees energy for *forgiveness*. Forgiveness unblocks the *love* at the base of all feeling. The pyramid looks like this:

Anger is a reaction and a defense against hurt. As children, we were easily injured because we were so vulnerable and had few protections. Feeling hurt made us mad. When we didn't get the comforting we needed, our helplessness also made us mad. Hurt that is not expressed converts into animosity. If our habitual response to a difficult situation is anger, it is important to identify what feelings are hiding underneath our anger.

No one likes *hurt* because it shows how vulnerable we are. We can try to defend ourselves against it by pretending we aren't hurt or denying that we have been hurt, which will only produce suffering and depression. In contrast, expressing our sadness releases our hurt. Many of us believe tears are embarrassing, so we suppress them, yet our bodies are designed to cry away heartaches. We rarely weep enough, especially for vague wounds, like not getting enough attention. So hurt remains undissolved. When we let ourselves feel the pain connected to specific incidents, we can let it go.

Once we voice our hurt, we get in touch with the *fear* below it. We fear being abandoned, being engulfed, and not being understood or loved. Children experience apprehension because of their frailty and dependence. Father-wounded people often don't feel safe. Fear is designed to help us be cautious or avoid danger, yet being habitually frightened shuts us down. It costs us the willingness to risk seeking satisfaction and adventure. Antidotes to fearfulness include talking about it, obtaining more information about our choices, finding support, and acting in spite of the fear.

What we fear most is that our *needs* won't be met. The raw, intense cravings of children are like the feelings of young birds who, with wide-open mouths, are waiting to be fed. We were totally dependent on others back then for survival, nurturing, and love. We were powerless to fill our wants alone. Once we accept how deep and wide-ranging our unmet needs were, we can take action to gratify them now.

When we realize what we had to do to survive, it becomes easier to *forgive* ourselves for failures and character flaws. Understanding the depth of our deprivation can produce compassion for ourselves. Once we perceive ourselves more clearly in light of our father-wounds, we can also step back and see our fathers in terms of their own injuries. If we can pardon ourselves, we can also pardon our dads. Would we be much different from them if we had a similar upbringing? Weren't they also damaged as children? Grasping this fact makes it easier to open ourselves to forgive them.

Working through the layers of our feelings about our dads clears the way for **acceptance** of our fathers and the situations we endured. Coming to **peace** with the past allows us to open to **love** – for ourselves and others. Some of us may love our dads once again. It is a tragedy to remain frozen in resentment against our dads when we could get in touch with our affection for them. However, that bond is not always present. Some men had no sense of caring or responsibility when they fathered children. Accepting this absence of connection can free us to move on to loving those who are available to us.

The more we're aware of the interconnections between each feeling layer, the less likely we are to stay stuck at any one of them. By expressing the sentiment above or below it, we can generate emotional movement. For example, if we're locked in hurt, we can work to express our anger or find out precisely what we fear. Releasing suppressed feelings liberates energy for us to do what we want with our lives.

> **The truth will set you free –
> but first it will make you miserable.**

WRITING TO DAD

Writing is often a very different experience from speaking, encouraging you to stay focused, think clearly, and dig deeper. A powerful healing can come from composing a letter to your dad. This is an effective way for you to get in touch with and relieve pent-up emotions. What follows is a letter that I wrote to my father. I intentionally incorporated all the levels of feeling, in sequence – anger, hurt, fear, neediness, forgiveness, and love.

Dear Daddy,

I am angry at you for leaving me when I was only fourteen months old. You died and left all of us, and mother never did recover from it.

Of all the kids, I was the one who was most impacted by her depression and her feeling burdened. She turned to me to make her happy, and I couldn't do it. I'm angry that you left me alone with a mother who was so lonely and critical. I'm angry about all the times that I needed a dad and you weren't there.

I'm hurt that you left me. Didn't you care enough about me to stay and see me grow up? I'm hurt that I never knew you.

Because I wasn't taken care of by you, I'm afraid that I'll never feel taken care of. I didn't experience you sticking it out with me, so I'm afraid that I won't have a man in my life who will be there for me and with whom I can be truly intimate.

I really needed a daddy. I needed you to play with me, to hold me, to tell me stories, to show me how to fix things. When mom was hard on me, I needed someone to be on my side sometimes.

I needed you to like me, so that I could believe that other people would like me too, especially men. I often felt as though I'd done something wrong, so I learned to be very quiet and withdrawn. I needed you to let me know that you liked who I was becoming.

I forgive myself for taking so long to recover from losing you. I forgive myself for all the time I used up being depressed and lonely. I forgive myself for having to learn lessons the hard way. It's taken me so long to find out that I'm a good person, and that I have something to contribute to others.

I forgive you for dying, Daddy. I don't think you really wanted to die. You missed so much by dying: some hard times but lots of good ones. You missed seeing us all grow up. You missed knowing how much I loved you, how much we all loved you. Mother misses you so much. She told me about the special house the two of you were planning to build when you retired.

I love you, daddy, and I know that you love me. I hope there is some way that you can see me or know what's happening to me now. If there is, I'm sure that you approve of me and love me. I know that I love you. Maybe someday, in another dimension, we will meet, and I'll finally get to know you.

Your daughter,
Jane

EXERCISE 12.   LETTER TO YOUR FATHER

Getting yourself to sit down and do the scary task of writing to your father is worth the effort, because the release of emotions can be so great. If you discover you have difficulty completing this assignment, I suggest that you find a partner who also wants to write to his or her dad. When you meet, set a timer for half an hour, and agree to keep writing until the buzzer goes off. If you don't have a father-loss buddy, then get someone else who is willing to work on a different project at the same time you are drafting your letter to your dad. It can feel safer to write to your father with someone nearby.

Tell your dad in a letter what's in your heart: all your anger, hurt, fear, needs, forgiveness, and love, in that order. This is your chance to write anything to him that remains unexpressed. Don't worry about spelling, punctuation, or your literary style. It doesn't matter if your letter is polished or not. Let whatever is inside come out.

Your writing pace may vary – sometimes the phrases will come to you faster than you can put them down. Other times each word will emerge with painful slowness. Just descend patiently through to each succeeding layer. Let your ideas emerge unimpeded. Your letter could go on for as long as twenty pages or be done in one. If nothing occurs to you, write about why you think you are drawing a blank. If you didn't know your father, tell him what your life was like without a father. Do not censor yourself. You don't have to actually mail this communication.

After you finish the letter, read what you have written out loud to at least three people. Ask them to listen without judgment or advice-giving. The whole idea here is to express your emotions, letting them flow from your heart. Each time you present your letter, allow yourself to re-experience and let go more of your feelings. Another person hearing and recognizing your pain is deeply gratifying. You feel accepted, relieved, and released. When I read my letter aloud, my voice catches and quivers, and I realize again how profoundly I am affected by the absence of my father. Each review can be another important step through the grieving process.

You may want to send all or part of this letter to your father. If he is dead, you can go to his grave or out in nature to read what you have written. If your dad is still alive, I recommend that you put the letter aside until you have completed the exercises in the next section. Then go back over it and decide if you want to mail or read any part of it to your dad. The feelings that were appropriate to express when you were writing may not be what you want him to hear after the intensity subsides. Give yourself a cooling off period, and then follow your intuition.

YOUR FATHER'S SHAME, YOUR SHAME

A father who feels good about himself can admit his mistakes to his family. The self-confident dad apologizes when he acts inappropriately. However, when a father has low self-esteem and cannot tolerate his own faults, he is likely to project his underlying self-condemnation on his wife and children.

Everyone has assets and deficiencies. People are a mixture of roses and garbage. A dad who won't admit his fears and failings tries to pretend they don't exist. He can't tolerate imperfections in his children, because they remind him of his own inadequacies. To keep his garbage safely buried, he makes fun of his son or explodes at his daughter. He belittles or berates the child in an attempt to remove the focus from himself and avoid his own troubled feelings. Without realizing it, he may perceive his offspring as a little trash-can where he can temporarily dump his fear, anger, or shame. Most often, the youngster takes responsibility for dad's upset, believing, "It's my fault. Since dad is good, I must be bad." The shame is transmitted from father to child.

Babies are naturally shameless. Only when little ones are teased, critically judged, or humiliated do they learn to be ashamed of themselves. The painful emotion of shame carries the sense that there is something fundamentally wrong with you as a person. With guilt, you know you've *done* something bad. With shame, you feel that you *are* bad.

A child often needs correction and guidance, yet many a dad condemns rather than suggests alternatives. Through wagging his finger, angry stares, or shaking his head over "hopeless" shortcomings, he passes his own feelings of inadequacy onto the youngster. He makes cutting remarks, such as, "Shame on you!," "What's wrong with you anyway?," or "Why are you so stupid?" Such words and gestures undermine a son or daughter's basic sense of self-worth.

you're stupid

If your dad put you down, you may have felt as though you couldn't do anything right. Perhaps you thought he would love you if you could only be how he wanted you to be. You might have been able to correct mistakes or adjust your behavior, but you could not change your nature. Shaming inevitably causes distress and despair. There is no constructive value in a generalized sense of shame. It is a life-denying self-attack.

If you have taken on your father's shame, it does not belong to you. You can symbolically give it back to him. It's like cleaning out your garbage can, putting a lid on it, and posting a sign that reads, "No Dumping Here."

EXERCISE 13.   GIVE SHAME BACK

This exercise contains a series of steps that dig down to the deep roots of your shame. You may want to set aside extra time to move through the following progression, which will help free you from the grasp of a strongly ingrained feeling of humiliation.

First, get in touch with your internalized sense of shame by answering these questions.

- Do you feel fundamentally flawed and defective?

- Do you cover up your true nature because you think you're worthless?

- Do you keep yourself isolated, feeling empty and alone?

- When there is a misunderstanding, do you automatically assume you are wrong?

Because so many father-loss adults are burdened by excessive self-reproach, it's important to determine how much of your shame originated with your dad. Don't be fooled by his apparent confidence. Inflated self-importance could have covered up his negative self-image.

Next, ask yourself these questions about your father.

- Did my dad seem to have a core of shame?

- Did he whitewash his sense of deficiency?

- Did he transfer his disgrace to me by raging, teasing, or criticizing?

- Is the humiliation I feel my own, or am I actually carrying and acting out what is part of him?

Now you can hand back the coat of shame to your father. Write out a list of the ways he shamed you. Give as many completions as you can to the sentence, "Dad, you gave me your shame when you..."

For example, "Dad, you gave me your shame when you teased me about my body... when you yelled at me irrationally the time I lost my jacket... when you compared me to a dog... when you expected more of me than any child could do..."

Then envision him standing fifteen feet in front of you, so you have to holler for him to hear you. Start hitting a large pillow or bed with a tennis racket or similar implement. While you are pounding with all your might on the surface in front of you, shout out, *"Dad, I give you back your shame! It doesn't belong to me. It never did. It belongs to you. I give you back your shame of never being enough! I give you back your shame for not being perfect!"* Name the shame he put onto you. Being careful to protect your throat from becoming hoarse, keep yelling these words, until you gain the sense that you have begun to release these harmful, contemptuous feelings.

Dad! Take back your shame!!!

Where applicable, you can also give back other emotions that properly belong to your dad, such as his anger, hopelessness, or neediness. You may have absorbed his fear, intolerance, or defensiveness. Start with the same phrase, *"Dad, I give you back your..."* Fill in whatever emotion you now realize you have been carrying for him.

If this process seems intimidating, you can work into it by taking smaller steps that build on each other. For example, first you can just pound the pillow. Then continue hitting, adding words at a normal voice level. Finally, while still striking, you can yell out what you're giving back to your dad.

Standing up to your father might feel foreign to you. You may have to do this exercise several times before you start sensing your own power. In the meantime, you can rely on the "act as if..." principle you used in expressing anger. You *act as if* you feel confident and strong in relation to your dad, until you do.

As you are clearing out physically, psychologically, and spiritually, you may also have an urge to clean out your closets, drawers, or the garage. Throwing or giving away items is a cleansing process that parallels the inner purging you're going through. Don't be surprised if you find yourself beginning such tasks at this time.

When you do the exercises in this book, you will change. Your emotions will churn up. You could find that you are not sleeping as well as normal. All this might tempt you to decide that this workbook project isn't worth the stress, so why go on? These are natural and predictable resistances. They mean your transformation is actually happening!

Learning about yourself is unsettling. Whatever feelings emerge, allow yourself to experience them. Note and be curious about them, then persist in the healing process.

Possibly none of these discomforts will arise. You might feel excited about what you're learning and want to share your insights with friends. That's great. You're growing in that case too, encountering yourself at a deeper level.

SECTION THREE

REAPPRAISING YOUR FATHER

By expressing your hurt and anger, you took a crucial step in discharging negativity toward your father. Exploring your dark side is essential preparation for moving into the light. Considering what you experienced as a child, it is appropriate that you hold your dad accountable for any pain he caused you – whether or not he realized what he was doing. You have the right to feel sad for the abandonment and loneliness you suffered, the times you felt neglected, misunderstood, or abused.

Nonetheless, as you reconnect with your memories from the past, you may want to re-examine some of these long-held attitudes. When you were little, you may have misperceived your dad's behavior, experiencing him as worse than he really was. If you reserve your understanding only for your childhood hurts and resentments, you can get stuck in justifying your own feelings and be unable to move on to compassion and forgiveness.

On the other hand, you may be so accustomed to your dad having the authority of "father" that you are extremely receptive to his pain. You could feel you owe him concern, or even believe that you should unfailingly respond to his wishes. If you feel too sympathetic toward your father, you can invalidate or bypass your own anger and sadness, winding up emotionally blocked. One woman said, "I have always understood my dad's position, but I didn't have my own reality. I understand him, and I still hurt." The key to moving ahead is to empathize with both the child you were *and* with your father.

ADOPTING A NEW PERSPECTIVE ABOUT YOUR DAD

No one had a perfect father. Each was a complex man who had his own history and aims. As a child you were only part of your dad's life, which was filled with many other relationships and challenges. Your father had an existence that in many respects was separate from you. It's often difficult to accept this emotionally, because your dad was so very important to you at the time.

As a youngster, you may have happily waited for the moment he came home. Meanwhile, he had to handle demands from his boss, spouse, friends, and other children. He dealt with his work, bills, household responsibilities, and community activities. All these tugged at him and competed for his time and attention.

Your father also had his own father, who greatly influenced him and – for better or worse – was *his* model for how to be a dad. Sins and tragedies typically pass from generation to generation. Often I hear that a troubled client's father's *father* died at an early age or was an alcoholic or abusive to his child. Everyone can benefit from investigating the family history. Learning about your father's parents and grandparents can help increase your tolerance for his failings.

It's very difficult for fathers to give more than they received. Knowing this, it's easier for you to look at him not only as your parent, but as a human being who repeated what he learned and did what he felt he had to do. He was a link in a generational chain of dysfunction. Ultimately, it's important for you to accept your father as someone who had strengths, limitations, and inner wounds – similar to yours.

STANDING IN YOUR FATHER'S SHOES

In order to see matters more clearly from your dad's point of view, you can stand in his shoes for awhile. You can do an exercise in which you pretend to be your father explaining himself to you. It might amaze you to discover how much you've actually sensed at a deep level about your dad. You may have resisted admitting to yourself how much you already do understand him. Some of this avoidance is self-protective: it hurts to connect with the pain of those you love.

Acting the part of your dad may enlighten you on why he did what he did, what he thought were his successes and failures, and how he lived with his hopes and fears. People I've worked with tell me that role-playing their fathers has also provided them an incredibly powerful tool for understanding their own behavior, because they realize their tendency to repeat their dads' patterns.

Deep inside, you may have hoped that some day your father would ride in on a white horse, slay the dragon, and rescue you from life's perils. Understanding him better is likely to destroy your remaining illusions that he will yet become the father you always wanted. A part of you may wish your dad could stay on a pedestal. Growing up means surrendering the fantasy image of your father as your potential savior.

To give you an example of how the process of standing in your father's shoes works, I'll begin with my own version of my father speaking to me. Because he left so early in my life, my direct experiences with him were probably less difficult than those you had with your father. The interpretations and feelings of an absent father will be quite different from those of dads who were abusive, judgmental, or distant. This is what I imagined my dad saying to me:

My dear little Janie,

I didn't want to die. I knew I had a bad heart, but I didn't let it stop me from doing anything that needed doing. There was always so much to do, and the filling station was cold and drafty, but I didn't think that I had a choice. I know now I was wrong.

There were times when your mother would make me so angry, that I'd go inside myself so I wouldn't explode. Your brother and sisters would make me mad too. They just wouldn't listen to me until I started yelling and losing my temper. I'm sorry about that now. I just didn't know another way then. My father used to bellow at me the same way.

Those last few weeks before I went to the hospital, I could hardly breathe when I got home. I'd have to sit on the back steps and rest before I could walk up the stairs to the kitchen. I started getting scared. I didn't want to die. I was young — only thirty-seven. The idea that I might desert your mother, and that she'd have to work and shoulder all my responsibilities, was terrifying. I put the thought out of my mind. I just had to get better. I couldn't die and leave all of you.

I know that your mother had a terrible time after I left. I'm very sorry that she had so much to handle alone. I also know she was hard on you. She demanded a lot. I'm sorry I wasn't there to act as a buffer for you.

I miss you so much. You were so sweet and innocent. You were my baby. There was a special feeling between us. I wanted to hold you and have you know that I really cared about you.

I would have been so happy at all your graduations. Who would have thought you'd get a Ph.D.? My buttons would have popped at that event, I'd have been so proud.

I'm sorry you've had such a hard time with men. Maybe that too would have been different if I'd lived. I want you to find someone who loves and respects you. When you meet him, tell him your dad says he's lucky, and he'd better treat you wonderfully.

I'm so sorry. I missed so much. I know how you all suffered because I wasn't there. I wish I could have been around to help you through the hard times and to share the good times. I'm proud of my family.

Janie, I love you. I want you to know that deep in your heart. I want you to feel my devotion, so that you'll never be lonely again. I want you to have a wonderful life, and I want you to think of your father from time to time. He loves you.   Daddy

---

EXERCISE 14.   YOUR FATHER TALKING TO YOU

The purpose of this exercise is to know your father at a deeper level and to get in touch with parts of him that he doesn't or didn't readily reveal. As an adult you don't have to be satisfied with the lack of personal communication you may have experienced growing up with him (or without him). Through role-playing, you can get him to tell you how his childhood influenced him, why he treated you the way he did, and how he evaluates his own life. If you weren't well acquainted with him, invent what he might have thought, felt, or said. Perhaps you can call on family stories for additional images and ideas about your dad. If not, see what comes out when you use pure intuition.

For some, role-playing your father can reveal new explanations for his acting mean or abusive. But if what you find yourself saying, as your father, still hurts you, reach deeper until you get to his more vulnerable levels. At the very least, know that you don't have to take his harsh words at face value. If he gives you excuses, have him talk about his feelings.

This exercise may be easier for you to do if you schedule it at a definite time and practice it with someone else. Sit facing each other, holding hands. Alternating turns, take as much as

ten minutes apiece to role-play your fathers. If you do the process alone, either talk into a tape recorder or write out what comes up for you.

Begin to be your father. Sit in his chair, walk in his shoes, get

inside his skin. Look at the world through his eyes. Explain anything the healthy, honorable (but often suppressed) part of your dad would want you, as an adult, to be clear about. Get him to reveal the real sources of his pain.

You can get in touch with your father's motivations, hurts, conflicts, goals, expectations, heartaches, regrets, guilt, shame, and love. He might tell you about his parents and the traumas of his early life. What were the times like while he was growing up? What was he taught about how to be a man, husband, and father? How did his wife (or wives) affect him? What losses and crises did he experience?

Have your dad be more open and vulnerable than he's ever been, to make sense of himself to you. Let him own his feelings and take responsibility for what he did or didn't do. Right now, make a link with him and let him speak to the adult part of you from his heart.

"I found that my dad was not really a monster," was one class member's reaction to being his dad. "He ranted and raved at home, but I also remembered that he suffered a bad accident, was an epileptic, and used alcohol. He was afraid every day that he would lose his job if his boss found out these facts."

One woman confessed, "It makes my dad more human." Another considered, "At first I didn't know if I was just making excuses for him. Then I thought how would feel if I were in his exact circumstances. I felt sad for him. I never thought of him having fears."

"This exercise changed a fundamental misperception I had about my father," said a third woman. "I thought he didn't love me. With relationships, I'd find a man and try to figure out how to make him love me. I was battling the wrong dragon. Now I see my dad thought he was showing me love. It's just that his version was so different from mine."

Deepening Your Experience

Answer these questions in your journal.

- What did you learn by being your father?

- Were you touched or surprised by what he said?

- How did you experience your dad differently from before?

- Looking at him with more understanding, what did you notice?

- Did you have any unexpected reactions or insights to this process?

This would be a good occasion to do more research into your father's background. What do you know about his mother and father and his grandparents? Find out about the forces that shaped him: his religion, national origin, and family traditions, plus the social, economic, and political influences that colored his attitudes.

EXERCISE 15. PARENT YOUR FATHER

By imagining yourself being a parent to your dad, you switch places with him and gain greater perspective about him. He was once a little boy and still has a child within him. As his mother or father, you may recognize how many of his needs were not met.

This exercise can help you see how much you and your father shared the need to be nurtured. As his make-believe parent, your job is to provide for and cherish him. Please understand that this role reversal is different from the responsiveness to his wants that he may have exacted when you were a child. Filling your father's personal requirements, such as listening to his adult problems or being his private servant, was not your proper responsibility. This process instead involves a voluntary repositioning where you treat him as you might have wished he related to you.

If you could have influenced your dad as a boy, what would you have said or done? As his caretaker, how would you have contributed to his self-esteem and the development of his character?

_____

Imagine yourself as the parent of your dad. He is just a little kid, getting along in the actual circumstances of his life. As a loving father or mother, how can you support this child to grow into a well-adjusted adult? You could tell him what he might never have heard from his own folks.

See yourself communicating the words that might have made a difference, because you know the man he will become. You understand his strengths and weaknesses. You can encourage him to do his best and help him where he has difficulties. Like all children, he needs more than anything to know he is loved. Write to your father the words he needed to hear as a boy. This is what one class member said to her dad:

My dearest Jerry,

Even though my pregnancy with you came as a surprise, I grew to look forward to your birth with joyous anticipation. It was such a special and happy moment when you were born. From the start I loved and treasured you even more than I could possibly have dreamed.

As you grew and matured, and it became apparent that you had your dad's German temper, I knew I had a challenge to help direct that energy. You had so much forcefulness that it sometimes threatened me, but I could tell all along it would move you to do great things. I could also see how sensitive your little boy feelings were. That is why I prayed to God and drew on all the patience and wisdom I could tap, to keep from acting and speaking too hastily when you spoke up or often blindly charged ahead. I knew that with a lot of love and tenderness - and firmness too - all that potential inside you could be channeled to good and creativity.

You are so precious and special to me. I know you are self-conscious about your size, but I have never wished you were anything else than you are. You don't have to be tough or do anything particular to prove you are a man. Though we both became uncomfortable with me holding you as you grew older, I'm glad I was able to honor your boundaries and yet never pull back from you. I love everything about you so much.

Love,
Mom

Reflect on the thoughts and feelings that come up for you in writing your letter. It may show you how needy and damaged your father was from childhood on. His wound could have been just as painful as yours. Despite his limitations, he probably did exert himself to give to you when you were a child. As you heal from your own hurt, you might find within yourself enough generosity of spirit to see the source of your dad's suffering and be willing to comfort him.

RECLAIMING YOUR POWER FROM DAD

You have been trying out various strategies to increase your empathy for your father. However, you may experience resistance to adopting his perspective.

Perhaps you still think of him as more commanding than you. You may fear that if you acknowledge his pain, you'll lose your own hard-won independence. You may feel you must keep him from unduly affecting you. But remembering that his behavior was unacceptable ensures that you won't give away control to him.

While your dad has left his imprint on you, as a conscious adult *you can determine how much influence he has on you.* It's your choice. You definitely are in charge. You can understand him without being overwhelmed by him. In fact, you may be able to take back the power you routinely surrendered to him earlier in your life. All the resources you need to reclaim your authority are inside you.

You can help confirm your sense of personal power by re-imagining your past, leveling the playing field you and your dad are on. In the process that follows, you test out what it feels like to be strong in relation to him. You no longer stifle your feelings and opinions to appease him, as you probably did back then. This time you speak your truth instead of hiding it.

EXERCISE 16. PROCLAIM YOUR POWER

In preceding exercises, you expressed your anger, sadness, and yearning from the wounded child's position. At this point you can take one further step and tell your father the kind of treatment you believe you merited.

As a youngster, you probably took your dad's behavior for granted. You barely realized it could be any other way. You may have had little chance or ability to talk to him. Now instead of compliance or perhaps the rebellion of your past, you can simply assert yourself to him. As an adult, you have more insight into his life. You also have greater capacity to stand up to him, to express yourself. Your mature self can help your child self find the assurance to declare your wants and needs to your dad.

While sitting erect, with both feet flat on the ground, close your eyes and begin taking slow deep breaths. Breathe in through your nose and out through your mouth for three minutes. Take this time to make contact with your deepest, wisest self, as you become aware of your own strength and determination to stand up for yourself.

Now imagine yourself as a child facing up to your dad. Your adult self stands invisibly in the background, helping your young self to speak the truth. First, remember a few specific times when you felt ignored, abused, or unfairly criticized. Next visualize your empowered child clearly telling your dad what you feel, need, and deserve. You can also set boundaries by communicating to your father which of his behaviors are acceptable to you and which are not.

After this envisioning, write down in your journal what you expressed to him. Read over these phrases to get an idea of what you might say:

> *Even if you had a difficult life, Dad, and didn't get attention as a child, I want you to show an interest in me now.*
> *You've been hurting me, and I want you to stop.*
> *I want you to apologize when you've been unfair to me.*
> *I deserve more time with you, not just a few minutes when you can squeeze me in.*
> *I want you to listen to me when I'm upset or excited.*
> *When you're angry, tell me if it's about me or if something else is bothering you.*
> *I want you to tell me when I'm doing well and to let me know that you like me.*
> *During dinner, I want you to ask me how my day went and to tell me about your day.*
> *I want you to help me with my homework and read me stories.*
> *I want you to play with me and take me places you go.*
> *I want you to do projects with me and teach me what I need to know when I grow up.*
> *I want you to hug me, hold me, and tell me you love me.*

"I need to have you sober, so you can be present to listen, support, and guide me," wrote one woman. "I need for you to hold me when I cry and tell me that I'm okay and that God will help us. I need you to follow through on your promises. I also want you to reward and praise me."

Your new, more empowered attitude might even impact how your father treats you now. If not, remember his response is secondary to your taking initiative, claiming your power, and stating who you are and what you want.

FORGIVENESS

You have been entertaining different perspectives about your father to help you let go of fixed positions regarding him. Once you're more flexible, it becomes possible to consider *forgiving* him for the way he treated you, despite your suffering.

Pardoning your father is difficult because it requires a reorientation of the way you view the world. If you find yourself resisting absolving him, ask yourself, "What do I get by holding on to these hard feelings? What's in it for me?"

Forgiving isn't something you do only for the other person. The main reason for you to absolve your father is because *it feels good!* The pardoning isn't just for him. Your dad may have already died or be very old. It's for you. Walking around with bitterness and spite is counterproductive. Forgiving unblocks your energy. You move on to a healthier and more fulfilling way of being. You feel free and alive.

Hanging on to indignation keeps you locked into a position of judgment. Vindictiveness makes you rigid, keeping your verdict against your dad frozen inside. You remain wounded, incomplete, and in pain. Harboring ill feelings without dissolving them absorbs your energy, sapping your vitality and stopping power from flowing through you. By clinging to the past, you continue to recreate it.

One workshop participant was adamant about saying, "I *understand* my father, but I don't want to *forgive* him, because I don't want to open up my heart to him." If you don't feel safe, you need not make yourself vulnerable to him. Forgiving and *not* forgetting is a protective way to interact with your dad.

HOW TO FORGIVE

Forgiveness begins when you let go of the hurt that you experienced as a child in your relationship with your father. You give up your resentment toward him. You make a decision to see your dad, yourself, and your past through compassionate eyes. You are not condoning your father's actions, which may indeed have not been okay. You are simply surrendering the victim role, adopting instead the attitude that, "In spite of what happened to me, I will be fine." As you allow yourself to relinquish your childhood pain, accept your father as he is, and experience more fulfillment in your own life, you can forgive more and more.

> **Some actions may not be forgivable, but people usually are.**

If you separate your father's *behavior* from his *essence*, pardoning him becomes easier. In situations where abuse occurred, it is particularly important to find out whether your father was victimized as a child. In a high percentage of cases, he too was part of a continuous cycle of dysfunction. You can comfort yourself with the knowledge that by committing yourself to this emotional and spiritual healing work, you are changing a destructive family pattern.

Having stood in your father's shoes, it will be easier for you to understand that the reason he didn't provide you what you needed is that he didn't have it to give.

Yet in his limited ways, he supplied what he could. To not acknowledge what he did offer you because you wanted more is to deny what you got and miss who he was.

Forgiveness also involves owning responsibility for your youthful feelings and actions. Have you been basing your current attitudes on a child's distorted view of events and motivations? A friend of mine was resentful for years that his older brother was his dad's favorite. He recently realized that though his father may indeed have preferred the brother, his dad nonetheless did love his younger son a great deal. My friend had been so distressed about being second that he minimized just how much guidance and support his dad did give him.

In what ways did *your* behavior contribute to the pain in your interactions with your father? Children can be very insistent on having their needs met on their own timetable. Clearly, all youngsters drive their parents crazy on occasion. A little boy or girl asking for a sixth piggyback ride can tire even the most generous of dads. Think of all the times teenagers ask for money, the car, and later curfews, or play loud music, talk on the phone interminably, and get into trouble.

Even more tellingly, a child often purposely provokes his or her father, goading him into a rage, by doing exactly what s/he knows will bother him most. If the father overreacts, clearly some portion of blame falls on both the child and the father.

Once you recognize your degree of accountability, it is important to pardon yourself for these childish mistakes. Whatever part you may have played in your troubled relationship, essential to forgiving your father is to forgive yourself. The judgments you make about him are similar to the ones that you're holding about yourself. Until you lighten up on yourself, it's hard to let him off the hook.

But what happens when you try to forgive your dad and you can't? For some, the pain is deeply entrenched because the wound was profound. Perhaps the effects of a father's alcoholism were devastating, or he physically or sexually abused his children. Though you've tried various approaches and gotten some relief, the bottom line is that you simply cannot let it go. Some conduct is extremely difficult to pardon. This can be discouraging, but you *needn't lose heart*.

Sometimes the wound heals in its own time, not yours. Even though you substantially recover from damaging fathering, this remains a life-long process. Painful emotions related to dad are likely to re-emerge during certain developmental stress points, such as job changes, getting married or divorced, or having a child. An attainable goal is to minimize the influence of your father-loss on your life, reducing it from a stabbing ache to a twinge of regret. As you keep doing your best to release your feelings and forgive, much of your pain will ease.

EXERCISE 17. THE PROCESS OF FORGIVING

Forgiveness is a *process* of liberation. The more you forgive, the better your relationship with yourself and with your dad. You may find there are some behaviors you can exonerate your father for and others that you are not yet ready to release.

Please review the list of grievances you wrote out earlier in Exercise 8, when you completed the statement, *One thing I don't forgive my father for is...* **Regarding some of the items, you now may feel differently toward your dad, having experienced more of his point of view. For each of the complaints you noted, go back and ask the following questions:**

- **Why might my father have done what he did to me?**

- **Did I have any responsibility for or participation in the situation? In some cases, especially if your father physically or sexually abused you, you may have had no complicity, but in others you might be ready by this time to share the blame.**

Identify whether your attitude regarding any of these previously unforgivable offenses has shifted with your increased understanding. For some of his actions you may find that you can totally absolve him. For others, only partial forgiveness may be possible for you at this point. A few may seem just as unpardonable as ever. Accept whatever level you have reached. Write out this thought: *"I can now forgive my father for..."*

Visualize your father accepting your forgiveness. See him saying to you that he understands the pain that he has caused you.

"I can now forgive my father for raging," one class member wrote. "He told us how he had been beaten with a belt as a child, and he refrained from that. I know how hard he must have tried to be a better father than his father was to him."

"I don't see my father as the enemy any more," another student said. A third realized how much of her identity was wrapped up in her negative feelings toward her dad. She explained, "Hating my dad was a protection for me. As I let go of it, I saw my emptiness on the other side of the wall I'd built."

SEEING THE POSITIVE

Now that you have expressed and cleared out some of your worst feelings toward your dad and made progress in forgiving him, you can open your heart to recognizing his good qualities. Consider what your father did provide and how he favorably influenced your life. Acknowledge the ways that he showed you he cared about you.

Your father's shortcomings were in the foreground when you started this healing process. They can move now into the background, while his positive traits come forward.

EXERCISE 18.   APPRECIATE YOUR DAD

Start remembering actions that your father did for you that you value. Compose several endings to the following phrase, writing them out or speaking them into a tape recorder: *"Dad, I appreciate…"*   Give as many completions as you can. As more acknowledgments come to mind over time, you can keep adding to your list.

"Dad, I appreciate you teaching me to drive," recalled one class member. "You were very encouraging. You took me out in the evenings after you got home from work. I also appreciate the baseball games you took me to."

Another student had to go further back to find positive memories. She wrote, "Dad, I appreciate your reading the comics with me when I was two years old. You'd spread out the newspapers on the floor, and we'd sit on them and look at the cartoons together."

GIVING YOUR FATHER HIS DUE

After appreciating your dad, you may be ready for yet another level of positive recognition. You can *honor* your father. Perhaps in the past you underrated his strengths and exaggerated his misconduct or negative motivations toward you. There may be many ways he merits your esteem.

Honoring him means that you acknowledge his value, even though he had flaws or did an imperfect job raising you. You credit him for giving you life and for the benefits he did provide. You are to some degree his reflection, and it's important to prize those good traits in you that come from him.

Besides what your dad did for you personally, look at him from a wider angle, taking into account the whole context of his life and the assistance he gave to others.

- Was he a responsible human being?

- How did his friends and peers see him?

- What kind of worker was he at his job and around the house?

- Did he belong to a service-oriented church or fraternal club?

- Did he do anything of larger value creatively or for the community?

You can recognize him for his accomplishments as husband, provider, friend, member of volunteer organizations, and any other contributions he made inside or outside the home.

EXERCISE 19. HONOR YOUR FATHER

Make your testament simple and truthful. It is important to maintain your integrity, rather than push yourself to praise your father if you don't feel ready. On the other hand, this process does provide a lovely opportunity for you to speak whatever respect you feel. You may even be able to say to your father in person some of what comes up for you.

Write down or tell your tape recorder how you honor your father. Using your dad's first name, complete the following sentence: *"I honor my father, (state his name), for ..."*

One workshop attendee wrote, "I honor my father, Arthur, for being decent and law-abiding and God-fearing and country-honoring, and for stopping drinking twelve years ago and finally giving me a dad I can love so much and be so proud of." Another honored her dad "for getting all the help he could for my sister when she had polio and doing whatever it took to pay for her treatments and operations, going without for himself."

For what can you honor your dad? In many cases, he did give his time, effort, and money to you and others, whether he did these things particularly graciously or not. You will feel good putting into words your regard for him.

TURNING FROM THE PAST

Thus far, you have adopted your father's perspective, worked toward forgiving him and yourself for the trespasses of your childhood, and honored him for what he did give you. Now it's time to say good-bye to the *image* of your father you've been carrying around all these years.

You probably still hold on to some of your old expectations regarding your dad, wishing former times could have been different or hoping that one day he will change into the father you want him to be. As long as you continue to pine for what never existed with your dad, you will be stuck in the past. Releasing your longing for what you missed enables you to admit that your dad will never be the way you might have liked.

> **Healing requires letting go of what could have been in order to have what can be.**

When you forgo your dream-father, you make space to experience genuine satisfaction from the people and purposes in your current life. Renouncing unfulfilled desires takes a burden off of you. If you've been trying to find just the right key to open your dad's heart, so that he will love you the way you wanted, finally giving up that search is a great relief.

EXERCISE 20. A GOOD-BYE TO THE DAD OF YOUR YOUTH

It is important to say farewell to your old relationship with your father in order, at last, to leave behind your childhood hopes and fantasies.

You can best do this visualization exercise while sitting in a quiet, secure place. Begin by reading the guided imagery portion into a tape recorder. Be sure to speak slowly enough so that when you play it back there is plenty of time to picture yourself in the scene. Then start the tape and close your eyes.

Guided Visualization:

Imagine you and the father of your childhood taking a final walk together. First, decide what kind of day you want it to be. Is there a gentle breeze in spring? A baking heat in summer? A misty chill in autumn? A crunchy cold in winter? Perhaps he looks the way he did when you were little, or during your teen years. As you stride next to him, study his face, his hands, his whole being. What is it like to be in his presence? Note what feelings come up for you.

After you two have strolled for a long time, you come across an old-fashioned railway station. There's something inside of you that prompts you to go in and buy a ticket for yourself. You find out your train will be departing in just a few minutes.

As you and your dad wait on the platform together, you know you'll never return. Once you get on the train, you will be relinquishing forever this father who symbolizes all your unfulfilled childhood wishes. You look into his eyes and say, "Good-bye, Dad. I am going to leave you now." How do you feel when you tell him this? How does he react? Do you want to hug him? If so, give him a last embrace.

Now you turn away from him and get on the train. You find a seat by the window so you can look out at your dad. The train starts slowly moving. As it picks up a little speed, you continue to look out at him. You nod and wave. Then you watch him diminish in size, knowing that you can never go back to this father. Eventually, he becomes just a dot in the distance. Then you can no longer see him at all. Now you face forward. You are very still for a long time.

After a while, you begin to notice how beautiful the countryside is and how intriguing the other passengers look. You start to focus on yourself. You ask yourself, "Where is the train taking me? What plans shall I make for myself?"

Sit quietly for a few minutes, focusing on what has just happened in your imagination. Allow the idea to penetrate that you have surrendered the fantasy of having the father you always longed for. No more do you have to hope and wait for what he might be to you or give you. Once you let go of your expectations of him, what do you feel? Are you sad? Do you sense any relief? Now go back and create the answers to the questions you asked yourself earlier. Where is the train taking you? What plans will you make for yourself?

Whatever you felt, one of the hardest actions you will ever take is giving up the idea that your father will take care of you. With such a farewell, you can formally and finally complete your relationship with the dad of your past.

Deepening Your Experience

Write down your feelings regarding any sadness or fear you experience in letting go of the father of your childhood. In what ways will you benefit from releasing this vision of him?

Draw a picture showing yourself saying good-bye to this dad. Remember the option of using your "other" hand.

REVIEWING YOUR PROGRESS

Having earned a respite in your journey toward healing, this is a good place for a recap. Retrace the steps you've traversed in adopting a new perspective about your dad. Which of the phases listed below do you feel you've completed? Which ones need more time and effort for you to accomplish? Assess how far you've come in your development.

STAGES IN REAPPRAISING YOUR DAD

1. Acknowledge the ways in which you feel your father hurt or deprived you.

2. Release this negative energy by doing exercises in which you express from your heart your feelings toward him.

3. Accept your father as he is.

4. Forgive your dad for hurting you and yourself for any misdirections in your own life resulting from your reactions to him.

5. Look for the positive in him.

6. Value his merits and respect him for doing his best.

7. Say good-bye to the father of your childhood, so you can focus on loving yourself, fulfilling your life's purpose, and building more satisfying relationships.

The worst is over. You can breathe a sigh of relief. You have reached an important turning point in your healing process. Until this time, you've been struggling through a dark tunnel with the light always ahead. At last, your unrealistic expectations have died. You have completed the past by purging painful feelings. Now you can shift your attention to the present and future. You are ready for a rebirth.

The process of actively reconstructing yourself begins with rediscovering the precious baby within you. Looking for ways to nurture and satisfy your spirited inner child can be fun. You will find taking care of your deepest needs to be very gratifying. Realizing how deserving you are, you can allow rewards to flow into your life. The actual possibility of experiencing freedom and pleasure will energize you. The prospect of joy is like a wake up call to a new reality.

SECTION FOUR

HEALING THE CHILD WITHIN

You may have been neglecting an important aspect of your being – your inner child. One of the fastest ways to develop yourself is to make friends with and take care of the little person within you. When your young and adult selves work in unison, you can reach your goals with less self-sabotage. Rather than trying by force of will to attain your objectives, you tap into the creative potential of your inner child. This intuitive side of yourself offers you invaluable guidance on how to achieve fulfillment.

NURTURING YOUR INNER INFANT

It is often worthwhile to examine what happened to you during your first year of life. You may have unmet needs that go all the way back to infancy. Early deprivations can contribute to persistent loneliness, compulsive behavior, and an underdeveloped sense of self.

It is helpful to recreate for yourself in the present the elements of fathering you may have missed long ago as a child. One way to heal your inner baby is to imagine a loving father paying attention to and satisfying your primary needs.

Because you initially had experiences before you could think in words, you may not know how to voice your lack of trust, your sense of not belonging, or your feelings of emptiness. What you took in, felt, and knew as a baby happened on a physical and emotional level more than an intellectual one. Now it is difficult for you to find words to describe what was experiential and pre-verbal at the time.

As a beginning, you may be able to piece together a better understanding of your infancy by asking family members to share their recollections. Body clues, such as persistent shallow breathing, sighing, scowling, and chronic muscle tension, may point to early deficiencies of protection and nurturing.

It is easy for little ones to assume that they somehow "cause" everything. Feeling nearly at one with their parents, they believe they will receive what they want. When they don't get it, they imagine that they did something wrong. In my own case, I discovered as an adult that at some deep level I still feared that trying to get my needs met would make others go away, as my father did. I believe my toddler-self felt *I* caused my father's permanent departure. When I couldn't get him to come back, I felt powerless and guilty. This kind of magical thinking, with its sense of being responsible for your father-loss, can stay with you for years and undermine your basic sense of confidence and capability.

The presence of a devoted father greatly influences your babyhood. Along with mother, he is your main source of love, sustenance, and security. He also backs up and supports your mom, so she has time and energy to care for you. If your dad wasn't available during your first years, his lack of involvement deprived you and negatively impacted the way your mother related to you.

The idea for the following practice came from John Bradshaw, the well-known expert on family dynamics.

EXERCISE 21.   YOUR DADDY LOVES YOU

You can provide a good father for the infant in you by treasuring the little one inside. Hearing reassuring words now can evoke in you a sense of safety and trust. Imagine an *ideal* father saying loving expressions to the baby in you. It takes courage to risk experiencing the strong feelings this process may evoke.

In a calm and soft voice, speak the following set of phrases several times over into a recorder. Be gentle, while allowing a good dad's reliability and strength to come through. To get a further feel for "dad," you might ask a male friend to narrate

the taping for you. It's important to read s-l-o-w-l-y and to pause between phrases to let each one settle in. Then curl up in a cozy position, relax, and set your recorder right next to you.

Before you listen to the tape, visualize yourself as a tiny baby, all sweet, clean, and content. You are looking up at your mother, who is holding you, beaming and cooing at you. Now your father gently takes you from her. You feel secure in his strong arms. You see his warm smile and the comforting glow in his eyes. You sense how proud he is of you. You hear him express the kind of affection and comforting you needed from him when you were an infant. Play back the cassette.

Cross your hands over your heart while he says:

What a wonderful baby you are!
I'm so glad you were born.
Just remember, you're Daddy's precious baby.
You're part of this family now, and you always will be.
We've been waiting with a secure place just for you.
You belong here with us.
You're priceless. I love looking at you.
I'm going to protect you and make sure no harm comes to you.
Your daddy's going to watch out for you.
You're safe, my dear one.
I like being your daddy and cherishing you.
I'll also take care of your mother.
She'll have lots of time to be with you.
I love you, my precious child.
You bring sunshine into my life.
I want you to take all the time you need to grow up.
I'll put my work aside often to pay attention to you.
I'll have fun with you as you get older.
Playing together will be good for you and for our family.
We'll have plenty of great times together.
I'm so proud of you.
You're such a beautiful, special little child.
You are a blessing in my life.
You're Daddy's terrific little baby. You make me smile.
Daddy's here. Everything's going to be all right.
Daddy loves you.

After hearing these words, lie still and be with your feelings. Let them penetrate deep inside, so you can recall them whenever you need to feel a dad's support and love.

Do this process at least three times a week for a month. As this only requires a few minutes a day, you will still be able to work on other exercises. By repeating these expressions several times, you can create a half-hour tape that will help put you to sleep at night.

Deepening Your Experience

In your journal, answer the question: As far as I know, how well did my daddy support me when I was a baby and toddler?

With your non-dominant hand, depict yourself as an infant being held by a loving father.

HONORING THE LITTLE CHILD INSIDE YOU

There's a child within you who almost certainly did not get what s/he needed from daddy. Accepting that youngster as a valid part of yourself is essential to the healing process. Usually, it wasn't safe to show all her emotions growing up, so s/he learned to keep them under cover. Having to sustain this secrecy is like playing the perennially popular children's game of hide-and-seek. It's fun and you feel secure while you are concealed in a good hiding place, but unless someone eventually comes and finds you, you feel lost and forsaken.

> **It's joy to be hidden, but disaster not to be found.**
> **Psychiatrist D.W. Winnicott**

The more of yourself that you reveal, the more you become whole and connected to the life around you. When you don't pay attention to your inner child, it rebels and causes havoc in the form of procrastination, temper tantrums, and self-sabotage. Honoring your little boy or girl means allowing the emergence of feelings and desires that you may have long suppressed. As these wants come to light, they could indeed have a childlike feel to them. That's okay. They don't have to be rational or adult, but they do call for acknowledgment.

EXERCISE 22.   CHERISH YOUR INNER CHILD

Throughout this discussion, I'll be using feminine pronouns, but the process works equally well for men.

Remember that your child-self did not mature the way the rest of you did. If you step back and view your inner child objectively, you can empathize with her sense of abandonment and disappointment. Your adult-self can pay attention to her, comfort her, and intercede for her. She doesn't have to be alone or frightened anymore. You can envision taking care of her now in the way she needed nurturing from a daddy long ago.

How do you give love to someone who is afraid to accept it? You have to be very patient, remaining aware of why she is guarded. It's not surprising, given her experience, that she has difficulty believing in someone. She had flawed fathering, so give her credit for making the best of a difficult situation. Honor that part of you that protected itself by being cautious and holding back. Give your inner child time to find out whom she can trust and that the affection she wants is at last available to her.

Read the following guided imagery into a tape recorder. Go very slowly, adding pauses. Begin to release tension in your body by breathing unhurriedly and deeply, seeing your entire being filled with light and love at every breath. Then play the tape back in a quiet secure place. Allow ten minutes without interruption. You may want to dim the lights and play soft music to encourage a free flow of ideas.

Guided Visualization:

Imagine yourself as a little boy or girl. Remember a specific time when you felt lonely or afraid. How old are you? What are you wearing? Now see your adult-self lovingly approaching you as a child. First you chat and make friends, and then you offer to put her on your lap so you can hold and comfort her better. If she does not want you to pick her up, let her climb on your lap herself in her own time and way. Then hug her and tell her that you're on her side.

As the two of you sit with each other, begin to notice all the ways that this child is attractive and special. Study her face and eyes. You can forgive her for being reserved or apprehensive, because you know the influences that shaped her. Let her know that you appreciate her and accept her exactly as she is. Be patient and understanding as you request that she tell you about her hurts and fears.

Ask the little one to tell you what she would like from you now. Provide it to her if you possibly can. Thank her for being open and sharing her feelings. Say to her that you're sorry she had to go through so many difficulties. Assure her that the decisions and plans you make from now on will take her needs into account. Hug her again and promise her you'll always be there to love and support her. Tell her you will return to talk to her frequently. Finally, shrink her small enough to place her in your heart.

Healing comes from loving all of yourself. You are as valuable as everyone else. Parent yourself fondly. Don't judge yourself. Let yourself be who you are and protect your right to express your ideas and emotions. This child is your own. Let her feel beloved, with caring that comes from *you*.

> **Now write a letter to the little person inside you, explaining the many reasons why you like her, and how you are going to listen and pay attention to her. She needs to see *in words* that you cherish her. You might also record your letter onto an audio tape so you can actually hear the consoling phrases.**

The following is what one seminar participant wrote.

Dear little Paulette,

I love you and care about you. I like you too. You are a real sweetheart and almost always treat other people nicely. Before you were shamed into being shy, you were enthusiastic about life and interacting with people. I like the way you look — your big blue eyes are so beautiful. It makes me feel happy to look at you.

I am going to start taking better care of you, now that I'm more in touch with you and know that you need it. I'm sorry I haven't done that in the past. I will set up ways to remind myself to talk with you as often as once a day. I will ask you what I should do to look out for you better. I will actually do things that you need to support you, such as finding time for you, doing activities you like, and being with people who are good company.

Big Paulette

Deepening Your Experience

In your journal, answer these questions. What is my natural child actually like? In what specific ways can I pay more attention to my inner child?

Make a sketch of the child within you.

Create a collage of pictures of children that appeal to you, whose essence and glow match that of your inner boy or girl. You might blend in favorite photos of yourself when you were younger.

ENCOURAGING YOUR NATURAL CHILD

Authenticity, innocence, and natural beauty are the hallmarks of your inner child. Denying her costs you liveliness and spontaneity. Do you want more vitality? Then make friends with and take care of this little kid inside. She has the power to help you bloom as a person.

The small child within you is a primary source of your creativity. When you provide for her, she gives you back fresh ideas and joyous energy to carry them out. You can encourage her in the same way a loving father urges his youngster to show her capacities and approves of whatever she produces. Be good to this little one — praise, comfort, and reward her. Allow her to be childlike. Remember, she didn't receive all that she needed growing up. Help her find ways to secure what she requires now.

EXERCISE 23.   TEDDY BEAR

While you are dealing with sad, lonely, or scary feelings from the past, your inner child may want to hold onto something soothing. Perhaps there was a stuffed animal, doll, or pet you were separated from or wanted intensely and never received as a youngster. Why not have the father-part of you buy a special "comforter" for your little kid?

Some men find it hard to relate to the idea of using children's playthings to console themselves. There is very little cultural permission for adult males to do this. Yet I know of fellows who, while at a residential workshop where they felt safe and accepted, enjoyed carrying around stuffed animals. Their choices ranged from teddy bears to panthers, rabbits, alligators, and gorillas.

Find a teddy bear, stuffed animal, or doll that you like. Connect with the teddy and let it delight you. You can pretend that it is you as a child and that you are its father. Cradle or play with this soft creature in the tender and loving way that you wanted a daddy to interact with you. Surrender to the nurturing and healing of this contact. Know that you can hug this companion anytime you wish.

"A lot of pain and hurt came up from the past when I let myself really hold and cuddle my stuffed bunny. I wanted to push the hurt away while it was happening," a woman reported.

One lady had forgotten details about most of her childhood. She had to work to bring back her memories. As she shared, "I bought a doll that looked like me at age seven and sewed up a copy of my favorite dress of that time to wear. I need accurate props to do these exercises."

"I got an alligator with teeth," said a different woman. "I want the softness of a stuffed animal, but I needed something that would also express the anger I feel."

A client of mine has a little teddy bear about five inches high that she can easily pack into a briefcase or purse. She is terribly frightened to fly. When she can't go with someone else, Teddy becomes her traveling partner.

Often processes like this one produce bittersweet sensations: sweetness from the immediate pleasure, bitterness from the contrast with your early experiences.

Deepening Your Experience

What feelings come up for you when you play with a stuffed animal? Do sad emotions arise? Can you allow yourself to surrender to and just be with them?

EXERCISE 24. TOUCHES AND HUGS

Touch nourishes your inner child. Making sure you have hugs in your life is a way to nurture the neglected youngster inside. If you were not held and cuddled enough as a kid, you'd do well to make a habit of putting more physical contact into your life now. Your little child will be glad you did.

Touch is the most primary need people have. The raising of infants in orphanages during World War II showed that proper nutrition is not enough. Babies who were well fed did not thrive unless attendants also played with and cradled them.

The very act of hugging, which involves extending your arms and unshielding your chest, heart, and midsection, indicates that you are willing to be vulnerable and open to others. It signifies that you want to make heartfelt connections, to respond to and be cared for by other people.

TOUCHING YOURSELF. Make a point of sometimes resting your hand on your cheek, giving yourself a foot massage, or rubbing your neck and shoulders. When you feel a yearning for affection, try folding your hands over your heart. This is an especially good way to stimulate loving energy. Caress any part of your body when you wish to feel soothed and vitalized.

RECEIVING TOUCH. Be open to appropriate hugs and touches from others. Ask people who are close to you for an embrace when you would like one. Treat yourself to a professional massage from time to time. Therapeutic touch wonderfully fulfills your need for bodily contact.

TOUCHING OTHERS. Give yourself the assignment of touching and hugging other people more often. Physical

contact is especially important if your family members weren't very affectionate with each other. There are many ways to connect. Making sure you have permission to do so, place your hand on a friend's arm, squeeze a shoulder, or give a pat on the back.

Family therapist Virginia Satir has said that people need four hugs daily just for survival, eight for maintenance, and twelve for good health and growth.

Besides brief, friendly touching, some tender, non-sexual embraces with the people in your life would be very agreeable. Be aware that there can be problems here. If you were abused, are sexually addicted, or are not sensitive about personal boundaries, pay particular attention to your feelings as you are giving and receiving touch. You may have uncertainty knowing your own limits or the other person's. Let any hint of unpleasant sensations be enough for you to stop the contact.

However, when the touching comes from personal caring and connection, such hugs can be wonderfully satisfying. Experiment with how often and in how many different ways you can add appropriate touch into your life.

Deepening Your Experience

In your journal, write about your attitudes regarding touching. How much contact do you like for yourself and want to give to others? How do you feel when touching others and being touched? How can you incorporate more non-erotic contact with others into your life?

EXERCISE 25.   ACCEPT KUDOS

When adults reflect back a little child's good qualities and notice his or her accomplishments, the youngster's self-respect builds. Your child within will experience a feeling of greater self-worth as you allow yourself to be touched by others' positive comments. Seeing yourself reflected in the mirror of friends' approval, you can recognize more of your virtues.

Don't let internal blocks prevent you from enjoying compliments. If you didn't get enough attention and praise while you were growing up, you may crave recognition yet feel uncomfortable with it now. Or, you may barely let yourself hear the appreciation you receive, because your deep-seated guilt and shame keep you from feeling you deserve it. As you more fully acknowledge your value, you may start noticing more of the accolades people do offer you.

Enhance your self-esteem by becoming more attentive to the favorable words that others say about you. Your task is to listen to their praise and be open to what they tell you. Give yourself greater permission to accept and credit the positive remarks individuals make about you. Keep a "Kudos" diary where you write down these compliments. I store mine on my computer. I just bring up the file whenever I want to make an addition, or I feel the need to review my "bouquets of affirmative words."

One shy woman class member reported her response to this suggestion: "I've begun to simply say, 'Thank you,' when receiving a compliment, instead of getting silly or passing it off as nothing, as I used to do."

You have come into greater contact with your spontaneous and creative side, learned how to be kinder to yourself, and discovered new ways to allow yourself pleasure. By acknowledging and nurturing your inner child, you have acted as a sort of father to yourself. Now you can build upon and extend this self-fathering function.

Thus far in the healing process, you have been focusing your attention internally. Now you have reached the transition point into producing concrete changes in your external world. Once you have reconstructed your *self*, you can work to remake your present *life*, reconfiguring it to ensure that it gives you everything you need.

Moving beyond the limitations imposed by your father-loss, you can have much greater success in looking after your well-being and in your career. You can push back former restrictions. New attitudes and actions will help you fulfill your potential. What your own father didn't give you earlier, you can start to provide for yourself.

* All the drawings in this book are by father-wound workshop participants. They used their non-dominant hands to get in touch with intense childhood feelings about their dads.

SECTION FIVE

BECOMING YOUR OWN GOOD FATHER

Even though you had inadequate fathering growing up, you can learn how to be *your own* good father. As an adult, you have the opportunity to become your own best buddy, cheer leader, and guide. You can develop the kind of nurturing attitude toward yourself that a devoted father would show toward a child that he loves. You can enhance those aspects of yourself which encourage, approve, and celebrate you, providing for yourself the kind of experiences you needed and wanted from your dad when you were a kid. Despite having to deny many of your desires before, now you can fill them yourself.

SELF-FATHERING

Self-fathering works to make you feel safe, balanced, and happy. The key is to concentrate on those areas where your dad failed to support you and supply for yourself what he didn't. For example, if your father didn't protect you when you were growing up, you can make sure your home is secure, take a course in self-defense, or set clear boundaries against being abused or hurt.

Was your dad too overwhelmed handling his own personal problems to set limitations for you and teach you discipline? You can give yourself more structure. If your dad isolated himself, so that you became used to largely taking responsibility for yourself, you can make a point of seeking help, consulting with others, and allowing yourself the pleasure of collaboration.

Did your dad play with you, take you on family vacations, and challenge you to risk and have adventure? If not, you can find time and resources for laughter, recreation, and travel. Did your father not provide well for your family? Now you can make sure you find work that pays sufficiently, don't spend more money than you make, and have a financial plan for your future.

Loving fathers reward and give gifts to their family members. In the same way, you can deliberately permit yourself a well-deserved day off, buy clothes that feel good to wear, or occasionally treat yourself to an elegant dinner out. You can take care of your body, the same way a conscientious dad is concerned about the health of his child. Physical fitness and mental health go together. If you are feeling down or depressed, the quickest antidote is exercise. You can also love yourself enough to eat properly.

Becoming your own good father does not mean you give into your every desire and whim. Self-nurturing creates sensible guidelines for establishing healthy habits, as well as setting constraints against self-destructive behaviors. You permit yourself freedom within beneficial limits.

You encourage yourself in your career and in relationships. You acknowledge each great and small accomplishment in your life. You share your successes with others, as well as allowing yourself to be seen and acclaimed for your merits. In general, like a supportive dad, you can cultivate the habit of being gentle, forgiving, and loving with yourself.

EXERCISE 26.   BE YOUR OWN DAD

To be your own good father, you can accentuate those aspects of your inner self which sustain your self-esteem. Your internal father's support and reassurance will help you fill in your empty places, stand up for yourself, and go after what you truly want. A precursor to treating yourself differently is to *talk to yourself* in a new way, replacing hurtful words your dad may have originally said with loving statements he didn't make to you then.

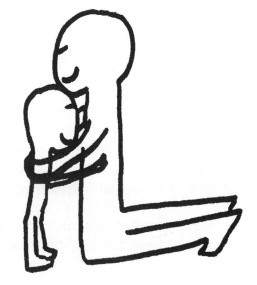

Redesigning your inner father has a powerful effect on the way you view yourself. In this exercise, you are reducing the impact of your initial memories by creating fresh, positive messages to yourself. Having given up the fantasy of what your actual dad should or might do for you, you no longer require his aid and acknowledgment. You're taking charge now.

Read the following phrases into a tape recorder and then play them back to yourself. You can also repeat them aloud during the playback. Replay or recite them three times a week for a month and whenever you need to inspire yourself. Add any other encouragements you can think of which have special meaning to you. Cross your hands over your heart as you listen to the good father in your heart saying the following:

I love you and I have confidence in you.

I will stand behind you – you can depend on me.

I acknowledge your many talents and capacities.

I want you to stand up for yourself. Your opinions and feelings are important.

I am proud of your accomplishments.

Have faith in yourself. I know you well enough to believe you can achieve your desires.

I support you and trust that you will succeed in what is important to you.

I believe you have a unique role to fulfill in this world. Others need your talents and your love.

I see your inner beauty, and I am deeply moved by you.

I trust you.

I encourage you to be a loving and sexual person who is passionate about your life.

I want you to enjoy your life.

I am proud to be your father.

I love you – just as you are.

I love you – just as you are.

Re-creating a loving internal father can help you maintain positive feelings about yourself. I know a public speaker who visualizes in her mind the father who died when she was a teenager. As she practices her speeches, she imagines him watching her from the audience. He smiles and nods his head and is very interested in and pleased by what she is saying. Then she sees him being the first one on his feet to applaud her. This image warms and heartens her.

GIVING YOURSELF PERMISSION TO BE ALL YOU CAN

One of a father's main functions is to give his child permission to be successful. Ideally, a dad supports his youngster in pursuing his or her interests because he believes s/he will be happy and proficient at them. A boy might like and show promise building models, doing science projects, playing soccer, or gardening. His father's enthusiastic faith that his son can do well gives him permission to stay involved and advance. For years my brother routinely took his three daughters to swimming meets. By giving so much of his time, he was saying, "I care about you. I want you to do your best, and I'm here to back you." His attitude helped one of his girls place in the California state swimming competition.

You needed a father to respect and guide you. His reassurance and praise were crucial in enabling you to become an effective person, to have warm, loving relationships, and to make your contribution to society. But your dad may not have given you this approval, even though you yearned for it. If you did not get sufficient backing from him, as an adult you may not feel you deserve to make good. Perhaps because you thought he would feel overshadowed by your accomplishments, you have been afraid to achieve more than he has. You take what comes to you, not having learned how to assume responsibility for creating your own happiness.

EXERCISE 27.   YOUR FATHER'S BLESSINGS

No matter how much encouragement your father did or did not provide, you can give yourself even more. You may be cut off from seeking what you want by believing that you can't have it anyway. Now you can confer on *yourself* the equivalent of your father's permission to effectively pursue what you desire.

This exercise is a guided meditation that will take about thirty minutes all told. It includes two parts, so please review the entire process before you begin. If you don't have enough uninterrupted time, you can do the recording in one session and the playback in another.

The first step is to tape both the deep breathing instructions and the guided meditation below. Read aloud slowly. Pause when you feel emotions stirring. Don't hesitate to re-record until you come up with a version that seems to fit both you and the spirit of the meditation.

The second step is to play back the tape, either right after you record it or at another time. Let yourself move into a quiet, receptive state of mind. As you do, open yourself to getting in touch with your feelings. Take in and make a part of you those phrases and ideas that are right for you. Let the thoughts that don't seem appropriate flow past you.

Relaxation and Deep Breathing Instructions:

(Begin recording.)

Put one hand on your chest and the other on your lower stomach, and as you do so, allow your eyes to close. Become aware of your breathing. Take in energy as you breathe in more deeply, then give it back out as you exhale fully. Feel the quieting in your chest and stomach as you inhale and exhale... Inhale... Exhale... Each time you exhale, allow yourself to become more relaxed. Permit your shoulder muscles to loosen. Feel your arms untensing. Let your hand muscles go limp. Allow the feeling of ease to spread throughout the rest of your body at its own pace. Relax... Relax... Relax...

Guided Meditation:

Dad, you didn't give me the blessings and reinforcement that I needed and wanted from you. Now I often hesitate to seek out the relationships and career opportunities I want. I see myself holding back because I am afraid to take risks. I didn't understand until now that I was waiting for you to tell me that you believed in me before I could go ahead.

Dad, I needed you to urge me to take chances in order to make my dreams become reality. I wanted you to tell me about the times you were afraid, when you made mistakes, and when you had trouble feeling confident in yourself. I wanted you to tell me that, in spite of your fears and your feelings of inadequacy, you went ahead and confronted the challenges you faced.

As a child, I wanted to know from you that I didn't have to be perfect, that you expected me to make errors, because that is how I would learn and grow. I wanted you to be involved in my school-work and my other interests. I wished you could like my friends and interact with them.

I would have liked you to accept the people I chose to love. I wanted you to be proud of me for being a parent. I lacked your guidance as I chose jobs and started my career. I needed you to trust that I could do whatever my heart was set on doing. I watched for you to show me that you were behind me.

My heart ached so often when you weren't there for me. I missed your understanding and endorsement. I grieve for blessings you didn't give me.

Dad, there were particular times that I longed for your love and support. I wanted to hear certain words from you on those occasions.

(End recording.)

Turn off the tape recorder and remain still. Contact the deepest part of yourself. Think of all the specific matters you want blessed in your life. Begin now to *give yourself* the permission and approval you would have liked from your father. Savor the feeling of receiving a father's blessing from yourself. Stay quiet for as long as you like, letting your emotions come up. Now write completions to the sentence: *"Acting as my own good father, I give myself permission to..."* Remember to let these declarations come from your heart as well as your head.

The capacity to realize your dreams has always been inside you. Believing in yourself empowers you. Success, security, good health, and fulfilling relationships start from within. That's why it is imperative to bless and encourage yourself.

Deepening Your Experience

Ask yourself these questions:

- In what ways do I hold myself back?

- What steps can I take to overcome my blocks and resistances?

- How can I give myself more permission to fulfill my potential?

FINDING YOUR PURPOSE

Certain people seem to know from early on what they wish to do with their lives. You may have had more of a struggle, seeking the right path but not knowing how to find it. It is the proper function of a good father to help his child gain insight into his or her talents. He also provides encouragement for his youngster to develop these abilities. But how many children had dads who paid attention to and supported them in pursuing what they liked and were good at doing? Without a caring father's input, you may not have gotten on a track that you could readily follow.

You are here to make your own unique addition to this world. Only by fulfilling your purpose for being can you find true satisfaction. But if you didn't have the kind of fathering that assisted you to make this discovery, it can be hard for you to recognize your gifts. The crucial factor now is that you believe that you have a specific contribution to make, and that you work to realize your calling.

Identifying what you genuinely *want* to do and noting which undertakings give you the most pleasure are the best criteria for finding your true purpose. Mythologist Joseph Campbell recommends that you "follow your bliss" in order to actualize yourself. The route you search out might not lead you where you expect. But pursuing whatever attracts you most will steer you to somewhere important. It may be only an intermediate step to revealing another direction. For example, my mother had the talent to be a concert pianist. She practiced long hours for many years to perfect her skills. But performing was too nerve-racking for her to actually enjoy. Giving up that course, she discovered she loved teaching children piano. She also gained great satisfaction from playing the organ in church, which she did for sixty years, from her late teens to her late seventies.

Once you follow your instincts by engaging in projects you love, your talent blossoms. That doesn't mean it won't take industry and patience to develop your aptitudes. Yet, when you're applying yourself to a labor of love, time seems suspended. You hardly notice as the hours pass. This intense involvement is one clue you're on the right track. When performing a task is filled with pleasure, the distinction between work and play blurs. Hopefully, you will be able to follow such a calling as part of your job. If not, you must find other means to fulfill your purpose outside your paying work. True *success* is discovering your special reason for living, taking on pursuits that serve your highest nature, and enjoying yourself in the process.

EXERCISE 28.   IDENTIFY YOUR DESIRES AND TALENTS

In order to realize your purpose, it's important to keep yourself open to messages that come from within you. Your intuition offers you answers, pointing you in the direction to go. The more you have released your anger and shame, the better receptor you can be. Sometimes you have to sit still and listen for your heart's desire. A voice deep within can keep you in touch with forces greater than yourself that may influence your destiny. Tune in to your internal promptings until you identify your proper role. Doing what suits you will ultimately bring you great satisfaction.

To put yourself in touch with your authentic desires and talents, place the following headings on three pieces of paper. Start lists under each title, adding several entries every day or two.

Activities I like doing.

Which of the ways you spend your time do you enjoy most? Write down all your enthusiasms, even if they don't seem related to potential work or projects. Your interests may involve family, love, and career, or athletic, recreational, artistic, financial, and spiritual endeavors.

Recognition I've received regarding my abilities.

The comments and compliments of others can be important clues to capabilities you may not perceive or claim. What you minimize or take for granted may amaze others.

Daydreams and fantasies that come to me.

Don't dismiss even the most far-fetched vision, since it could hint at or lead to a career track, passionate inclinations, or a path for self-development.

This process will train you to be more observant about yourself. After about a month, review the lists. Ferret through your urges, sifting for subtle traits and tendencies. See whether any practical directions emerge from all the items. Show this catalog to friends to gain their insight regarding possible projects or professions. Meditate and let ideas come to you over time.

Surprising opportunities may materialize from this self-exploration. Creativity depends on having the inspiration to see what is already there. Envision yourself taking a new tack. Picture how you would go about it, how you would feel doing it. You have the power to make it happen. Then try it out. Test yourself. Your bliss is at stake.

Every six months go back and check your lists. Identify any areas you have already experimented with and how the undertaking went for you. Highlight new fields to expand into during the near future.

One example of this self-discovery process in action is a woman who knew she liked craft projects, decorating for Christmas, and working with others. Friends and family remarked on her flare for design and color and her excellent organizational skills. She took an interior decorating course, which was interesting but not what she wanted. She dreamed instead of creating her own business. A year later she opened a small assembly shop that supplies department stores and florists with beautiful Christmas arrangements that she designs.

CONNECTING WITH YOUR HEAVENLY FATHER

Many people don't believe in the spirit or what they can't experience directly through their five senses. Others are absolutely convinced that a soul level exists. Paying attention to your spirituality gives you the ultimate experience of fathering. Assurance of your connection to Higher Consciousness, God, the Universe, your Higher Self, or whatever you wish to name it, offers you a profound feeling of support. Trusting to a Higher Power enables you to feel that your Heavenly Father is always available to care for and sustain you.

Your experiences with your own father color your religious beliefs. If your dad was kind, you probably experience the Heavenly Father as compassionate. But if you felt your father was unsupportive, harsh, or punishing, your idea of God may have been as austere, stern, and unjust. You could even deny the existence of any higher dimension.

Coming to peace with your past may open the possibility of your seeing the Universe as a more loving and abundant place. Until now, God may have seemed like an authoritarian father who judges you. In trying to pass muster, you could have taken on a set of strict moral rules that are difficult to live by. Operating under such a clear-cut system gives you a definite sense of holding on to something secure, yet there can be disadvantages. Stringent standards may lead you to evaluate your own and others' behavior in black and white terms. You could find fault with those who don't measure up to or share your values. You may become discouraged when you find that you yourself can't meet these high principles. Ever vigilant not to do wrong, you can fail to enjoy the present moment.

All the internal work you have been doing can bring you to a firmer assurance about your inherent worth. A more balanced view of your father will also make you generally more flexible and accepting. You can be easier on other people, rather than criticizing them because they don't fulfill your expectations. Your behavior can be based less on rigidity and control, and more on tolerance and unconditional love for yourself and others.

An acceptance of your spiritual nature is a key step toward being complete. Tapping into your spirituality can move you out of isolation and alienation. Feeling united to God from within, you need never feel abandoned again.

> **Your spirit, like a devoted father, provides a continuous presence that treasures, assists, and protects you.**

A consistently optimistic friend of mine points to the source of her cheerful temperament: "It's my philosophy. I have a deep faith that God is always watching out for me and guiding me." Few sensations are as gratifying as an internal conviction that the Universe loves and supports you.

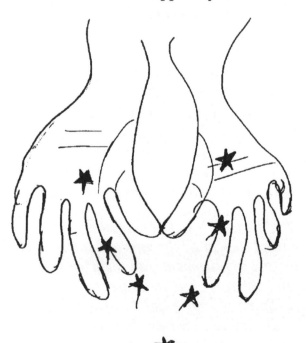

EXERCISE 2&. I AM LOVED

Being spiritual involves feeling an inner connection to something larger than yourself: God, Nature, The Light, Cosmic Consciousness. Coming to know that you have a divine force within you aligns you with the whole. You gain a sense of belonging to and flowing with the universe. This realization provides a firm foundation for inner peace.

To help develop your spiritual nature, record this passage on a cassette and replay it often. Establish the ritual of turning it on at the same place and time, morning or evening. You could also light a candle or play soft background music.

Because matters of belief are so very personal, you may not relate to the passage below. If it doesn't seem right to you, please use it as a springboard to find or write your own prayer or universal affirmation. The important factor is regular repetition with an open heart and mind.

Guided Meditation:

There are moments when I don't feel cared about or loved. I feel helpless and hopeless. I feel that I don't belong, that I'm not where I should be. What I need to realize is that loving is not primarily a matter of relating to others. The source of love is within me. I can develop an inner spiritual sense that I am loved.

I can acknowledge that I am connected to and cherished by the Universe. If I ever doubt this, all I have to do is go out and experience nature. Even living in a bustling city, I can look up at the sky and feel the breeze against my face. I can let the cosmos speak to me by walking along a shoreline, seeing the stars at night, standing still in a forest, watching the falling snow, jogging at dawn, or in any communion with the outdoors. If I allow it, all creation will touch me.

Despite not feeling fully loved by my father, I can come to know that I am lovable. When I look at all the gifts and talents I've been given, all my successes and accomplishments, all the friends and adventures I've experienced, then I can recognize that Life is on my side. I am sure that the more I open to Spirit, the more faith I will have in myself, and the more confirmation I will receive that I am blessed. When I trust that I am beloved, I naturally attract loving people into my life.

I believe deep within myself that I have been given capacities that are unique to me. The more I express myself and let the energy of the Universe flow through me, the fuller and richer I am.

EXERCISE 30. YOUR SPIRITUAL FATHER

You have a spiritual energy within you that offers virtually any answers you need. Your soul nature wants you to fulfill your highest needs and purposes. While your biological father is necessarily human and limited, you can always rely upon your Spiritual Father.

"Let go, let God" is a guiding principle you can follow, trusting in a Higher Consciousness than your ordinary awareness. You can involve your Spiritual Father in helping you remedy the dilemmas of your everyday life. Know that something good will come from your discomforts, even if you don't see the benefit right now. No pain or experience is for naught. You have the chance to grow and learn from whatever comes your way.

Write down three major problem areas that you are willing to turn over to your Spiritual Father. Asking for help from a higher source doesn't mean you just sit back to see what's going to happen. Spirit sends you energy, opportunities, and signs you can use to further your concerns. The cosmic support you receive generally manifests through what you do.

Each day review the predicaments you originally described. Be open for ideas to come to you about how to handle these situations. Watch how the challenges resolve. Look for the ways your Spiritual Father has assisted in the solution.

Note in your journal what you have gained as a result of enlisting the aid of Spirit in clearing up these three difficulties. This record becomes a physical proof for you of your Spiritual Father's participation in your life.

A twenty-six year old client of mine became pregnant during a rocky engagement. She was uncertain about whether to have the baby or to terminate her pregnancy. She prayed to her Spiritual Father for a sign to help her with her decision. Within minutes after asking, she switched on her car radio. The song that was playing was about the joy of having a child. Then driving through a normally busy intersection, there was only one pedestrian: a very pregnant woman, close to her delivery time. My client questioned no more, her decision was made.

One of the hidden advantages of a father-wound is that your pain and confusion often drive you to go within to find your answers. This tendency primes you to give your needs over to your transcendent parent. If you want to feel unbounded love, turn to your Spiritual Father.

Deepening Your Experience

Symbolize in a drawing your connection to God, the Universe, or a spiritual presence that is greater than you.

EXERCISE 31.   EXPRESS GRATITUDE

Much of your work so far has concerned the wounded child expressing feelings about how badly s/he was treated. While it is important for you to pay attention to that part of you, it is not the only aspect. From a balanced perspective, most of you did receive food, shelter, education, and probably much more. All these are reasons to be *grateful*.

Cultivating an "attitude of gratitude" can offset the negative tendencies to blame and feel deprived. It trains you to focus on the good as well as the painful, the benefits as much as the lacks. Even finding your way to the self-development process you are now undertaking is itself grounds for thankfulness.

This exercise deliberately encourages you to perform some very traditional activities you may have long since left behind — saying grace at meals and giving thanks before you go to sleep. Sometimes people get so hurried and sophisticated they think they can do without simple gestures of faith, yet these provide deep gratification. One of the best ways to realize how blessed you are is by adding up what you already have.

Before meals, you can thank God for providing you delicious food. Everyone can specify gifts that s/he appreciates receiving that day. This expression produces a beautiful tone of well-being that unifies the mindset of those at the table. Before going to sleep, take a moment to enumerate the bounty you have and acknowledge your gratitude. To give your thanksgiving more impact, light a candle as you recount the good in your life.

"If I could give my children just one gift, it would be to feel grateful for what they have," said an architect friend of mine. Gratitude gives you permission to enjoy your blessings fully.

Deepening Your Experience

Draw a picture of the people and circumstances in your life for which you are thankful.

Design a collage that celebrates who you are. You can incorporate pictures that represent your good qualities, what others like about you, your purpose in life, and your spiritual nature.

Damaging fathering probably left you with a harsh internal father. While shrinking him down, you have been building up a kind, loving dad within you. Becoming your own good father is the best way to step into your power. You are not looking for anyone or anything outside yourself to fulfill you. Instead, you understand that you are the ultimate source of your love and satisfaction. At first it may seem strange for you to think of being your own dad. But once you get used to it, self-fathering feels both stable and exhilarating.

Material, intellectual, and psychological gratifications cannot bring complete happiness. Recognizing your higher nature through connection with your Spiritual Father makes it possible for you to experience great contentment.

FINDING THE WISDOM IN THE WOUND

Father-loss teaches us valuable lessons. We can't change our unfortunate experiences with our dads. The challenge of our pain is rather to accept the past and find the good in it. We have the power within us to turn our father-wound to our advantage. The wound can be a wise one if it motivates us to turn inward to make full use of our resources of character. Many of our virtues derive from our adversities. For example, our suffering may have increased the depth of our compassion for others. The more we appreciate what we have become already, the more likely we are to transform our hurts into sources of value.

> **Our deepest wounds integrated become our greatest strengths.**
> **Delores Hart, Contemplative Nun**

MINING THE FATHERLODE

To reframe our ideas about the past, we can view our dad's effect on us through a new lens. What I call the "fatherlode" represents the internal strength we gain after overcoming the deprivation of inadequate fathering. We mine this fatherlode when we recognize the hidden treasures in father-loss.

We may even get to a point where we can see how our difficult dads were a blessing to us. If our lives had been easier, we wounded sons and daughters might have had less impetus to evolve. The discomfort of our pain pushed us to start on a journey of inner growth and keeps us striving to change. We can give ourselves credit for the courage that it's taken to go on developing, in the face of unmet needs.

Like a bonsai tree, we are each shaped by our experiences. The Japanese have made a spiritual exercise out of bending and pruning these small plants. The results of their art are often exotic and beautiful. In the same way, the hurts and lacks of our growing up years have made us special, producing limitations but also enlarging certain capacities.

EXERCISE 32.   THE POSITIVE SIDE OF FATHER-LOSS

This exercise clarifies how your experiences with your father turned out to be an asset in some manner later in your life. The trauma of inadequate fathering can have beneficial side effects. It's important for you to look at what you've gained as well as what you've lost. Acknowledging your strengths is a key factor in your recovery.

Growing up under trying conditions, you had to adopt various survival behaviors that could have been hard on you at the time. Later on, they may have turned out to be advantages. See how many of these qualities you can identify now. Fill in the following statement, *"Because my dad..., I..."* As an example, one student said, "Because my dad didn't give me what I needed, I became good at looking after myself.   I became self-reliant." Write as many completions as you can, incorporating all those interactions or deprivations with your father that ultimately resulted in strengthening you. Include worthwhile attributes or interesting life directions that you developed in response to your difficulties with your dad. Keep enlarging this list as new realizations come to you.

Various workshop members have noted the following valuable characteristics they felt they cultivated inside themselves in response to their father-loss experience.

"Because my dad was cruel, I went on a search to answer why people are the way they are. As a result, I have become more *spiritually aware.*"

"Because my dad rarely paid me any attention, I don't take being a *good parent* for granted. I want to give my child happy memories. Family times like holidays and birthdays are very special. I want Christmases like I didn't have."

"Because my dad criticized me severely, I learned *compassion* and a *desire to help others*, particularly those friends and people I meet who have been through similar experiences."

MAKING FRIENDS WITH SOLITUDE

One consequence of father-loss can be a fear of being alone. Solitude is a trial because it makes us confront our deep-seated sense of inadequacy and disconnectedness. Yet as we change our attitude about ourselves, it is possible to experience aloneness as a time for getting to know ourselves better and contacting our inner truth. The more we build our relationship with ourselves, the more self-sufficient we feel.

Inevitably, there will be occasions when we have to experience solitude. It's important to be able to tolerate these periods without feeling empty and cut off from the world. What a gift it would be if we learned to actually relish opportunities to be by ourselves!

We can start getting comfortable with the idea of solitude by first realizing that loneliness is just a feeling. Resisting it makes it harder for us. It doesn't serve us to hold on to such beliefs as, "I can't be alone… I need someone with me… I feel so abandoned… I keep busy all the time, so I don't have to feel anxious when no one else is around." Realizing that we influence what we feel by what we think, we can change our outlook on being alone and thereby reduce the power of such negative responses.

We have already discussed the value of acknowledging and connecting with our spiritual nature. We've considered reorienting our view of our Heavenly Father and felt the relief of asking for assistance with our problems from a Higher Power. Building on these experiences can aid us in other areas as well, especially in those situations where we feel we have no one else to rely upon.

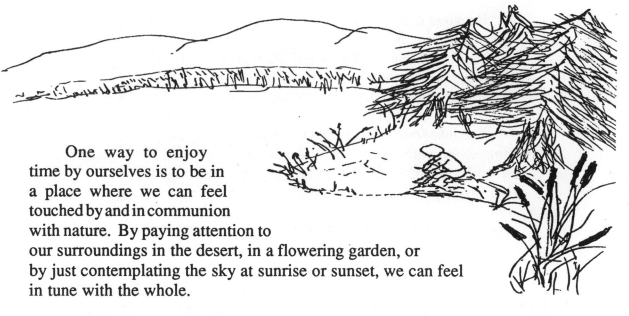

One way to enjoy time by ourselves is to be in a place where we can feel touched by and in communion with nature. By paying attention to our surroundings in the desert, in a flowering garden, or by just contemplating the sky at sunrise or sunset, we can feel in tune with the whole.

I remember what an enormous help it was to me in the last months of my marriage to walk and sit on the beach. My husband and I were engaged in a polite but painful conflict, a "civil war." Luckily, my daily route home from work took me along the ocean. I had never stopped there before, but during that upsetting period I would spend time at the shore almost every evening. I would look out to sea, often catching the last streaks of light at sundown and the first glimmer of the stars.

At first those moments alone would bring quiet tears, because I would let myself experience how sad I was, what a mess I believed I was in, and that I didn't know what to do. Then I'd feel calmed and reassured, sensing that there was some force grander and wiser than I which was watching out for my welfare. That was as close to a definition of God as I needed. I realized that whatever happened, I would be all right, even if it meant having to live alone again.

EXERCISE 33.   LEARN TO LIKE BEING ALONE

There are many other ways to learn to accept solitude besides contemplating nature, all having to do with going within yourself. When you were a child, you rightfully required and desired a father's concern. Now you can see that you no longer *need* him or even a substitute for him. All the peace and direction you want is within you. The following practices further develop your spiritual nature. Consider doing one or more of them regularly.

1. Practice Yoga.

Yoga is an Oriental discipline which involves specific body postures and an inward focus. Rhythmic deep breathing accompanies the movements. Yoga helps you to accept being alone, because it clears the mind and is very relaxing. It consistently provides you with feelings of self-sufficiency, serenity, and connectedness. It can bring you out of upset better than any tranquilizer.

Yoga is also a wonderful form of exercise, without the stress on ankles and feet that most aerobic workouts entail. It involves a slow opening up of the body that nonetheless keeps you fit. You can learn different routines from a class, book, or audio or video tape. It's simple to do. All you require is a mat and a small space on the floor or the grass.

2. Pray.

Another way to feel comforted despite being alone is to pray. Prayer is talking with God, expressing gratitude for blessings, and asking for what you need and want. It is a way of connecting to a Higher Force. Having to declare specific thanks and requests helps you identify just what it is that you appreciate and desire at this point in your life. Since you are addressing this Higher Power as another being, even when you're praying by yourself, you need not feel lonely.

The very act of speaking with a Consciousness greater than yourself implies some acknowledgment of its existence. You are affirming the belief that the Universe has the ability to help deliver your petitions. Yet you are willing to yield to God's larger wisdom regarding what is best for you. You feel linked with and backed up by this Presence who hears you and cares about you.

The power of prayer can be amazing. Over and over I hear stories of its remarkable results. When a friend of mine is in distress, his pet expression is that it's "time to hit my knees again."

3. Meditate.

If prayer is you talking to God, meditation is God talking to you. The process essentially involves "sitting quietly doing nothing" – in order to reach a receptive state that brings you to fuller understanding of and closer contact with pure beingness.

To achieve this level, you first practice calming yourself by slow, regular breathing, tuning into your inner self. Maintaining a straight spine is important, so psychic energy can flow easily between your sacrum and your head. To accomplish this, you can either hold your back erect, sit on a firm chair, or support yourself against a wall or vertical surface. Focus your attention onto your breath going in and out, a "mantra" like the Sanskrit word "Om," or a simple visual image, such as a triangle or a six-pointed star. This concentration of energy leads to a peaceful centeredness.

Another way to meditate is to ask about a practical concern you have. Just pose the question, sit quietly, be accepting, and see what ideas come up. Listen to the wisdom that flows from within. Write down your thoughts afterwards.

Meditation counters loneliness by showing you how emptiness can be a gift. Through this process, you free yourself from your mental chatter and surface preoccupations. You open up to an immense and wondrous depth which is always waiting inside you. Even ten minutes of meditation a day can transform you into a more harmonious person.

Deepening Your Experience

Which of the several methods for dealing with loneliness discussed above appeal to you most? Why? Will you commit to undertaking any one of these activities now?

Write about a time when being alone in nature, praying, or meditating helped you resolve a dilemma. For example, one man shared that after a week's backpacking trip by himself, he was clear which of two job offers he should take.

Draw a picture showing you satisfied and content in solitude.

EMPHASIZING THE WITNESS

A major reason we father-loss people fear aloneness is that we haven't felt a solid internal base of support and love. Deprivation from our early years has left us easy prey for suffering and self-pity. Our fragile sense of self has often been engulfed by exaggerated fears and doubts. We have tended to judge ourselves harshly, expecting more than we can deliver. Denigrating our capacities blocks productive energy and makes it hard to handle pressure well. We may have had the habit of retreating into avoidance and feelings of helplessness, rather than confronting the specifics of what needs to be done. Insofar as we were abandoned and shamed, we've had a tendency to become depressed when difficulties or overpowering emotions have arisen.

But now it is possible to come from a place of greater power. One way to work against discouragement is to develop a more objective attitude. We can learn to spot our inclination to feel defeated, saying to ourselves: "Okay, there's that negativity again. Where is it coming from? What does it signify? Why am I sensing it now?" Observing our feelings more dispassionately, knowing that they are vital but transitory parts of ourselves, is one pathway out of being victimized by them. We do not have to let our reactions overwhelm us and run our lives.

We can instead adopt a perspective called "the witness." When we're very upset, we can imagine that a part of us ascends to the ceiling and looks down at all aspects of our situation. We are often unaware of our capacity for this detached observation. To function as our own witness, we need to allow our higher consciousness to stand back and evaluate us with eyes of compassion and love. Fortunately, this level of self-awareness is built in, inherent, always there for us, whether or not we have paid it much attention in the past.

If we practice accessing this mindful facet of ourselves, we can avoid getting lost in self-condemnation or out-of-balance emotional states when our affairs don't appear to be going well. If we embraced a larger view, would we become so downcast and disparaging about ourselves? Odds are we would not. We would maintain more equanimity and be less prone to doubt ourselves.

The witness is essentially the same as the internal monitor which the Old Testament refers to as the "still, small voice" within. It often only speaks in a whisper. If we drown out this subtle murmur with negative attitudes like depression or self-criticism, we can't hear it. We've got to quiet down, lower the interior volume, in order to listen to a different voice. This steady, measured adviser can neutralize self-attacking tendencies. When the scope of our perception is wider, we can forgive ourselves more readily, the way a loving parent would.

EXERCISE 34. THE WITNESS

You can visualize yourself at any time taking the view from overhead. From there, you can get in touch with your broadest outlook and highest wisdom. This contact with your conscious self clarifies your vision, enabling you to assess where you are, correct your course bearings, and decide on how to proceed with integrity.

The purpose of this exercise is to gain a larger perspective about painful situations in your life, difficult decisions you must make, or events from the past that still bother you. Select one such troubling circumstance, then test out each of the following three ways to achieve the greater distance that will enable you to effectively re-evaluate your predicament.

1. Imagine that part of you has floated up to the ceiling. You're looking down at yourself, as from the dome of a

cathedral. You see the entire set of conditions that have produced the situation and your actions. These include being aware of how others behaved and how your past influenced what you did. You take the state of affairs less personally, so you can be clearer about what to do.

From on high, you can recognize that yours is but one of many dramas that play out every minute on this earth. In view of the whole, your problems may feel less momentous to you. Exercise compassion for your fears and needs. Acknowledge how misjudgments and doubt are normal and merely human. Be gentle with yourself. Feel yourself relax as you forgive the mistakes you have made.

2. To magnify this greater understanding, remember the kindest person you've known, and see how s/he would look at the situation. S/he might say, "No wonder you're upset. This is a difficult plight you're in... Of course you would have reacted that way... Almost anyone would have done pretty much the same thing... Be sure to take good care of yourself."

3. For an even more magnanimous vision, imagine an angel up there on the dome next to you. This being points out aspects of your dilemma you did not see at first, understanding you with the mercy and benevolence that comes from a cosmic and timeless contemplation.

Applying these new insights, see if you can consider and deal with your issue differently. Now pick two other trying circumstances and use the same overviews to reinforce this technique within you.

Contrast this perspective with the way you've been judging your actions up till now. Can you see how your old tapes tend to be debilitating, leaving you little space for self-acceptance? If your disapproval has been nearly automatic, it's time to forgive yourself for errors, previous stubbornness, or blind spots.

"Learning to see my past mistakes dispassionately, understanding that I did the best I could do with my then limited insight, helps me overcome my tendencies to punish myself and others," observed one class member.

Deepening Your Experience

Draw a picture of your own personal "witness."

SELF-LOVE

The wisdom of the wound can provide a doorway into self-love, all the more appreciated because it took a long time to get to and was not easy to reach. Seeing how our injury has affected us gives us compassion for ourselves. The point is to embrace ourselves *with* the wound, rather than warring against it or even just tolerating it.

Years ago, I believed self-acceptance was simply not possible for me. I was so critical of myself that any success I experienced brought me up no higher than the "maybe okay" category. Once I started recovering from father-loss, I was often surprised to hear myself saying, "I'm really happy!" I'd discover myself thinking, "I'm the luckiest woman in the world." I would feel this way while I was leading a workshop, swimming, working on a project, or seeing a good movie. I now feel assurance that I have value, and that joy is possible for me.

The following anecdote offers an exemplary attitude for maintaining our self-love in the face of our imperfections. A friend's mother always worked rapidly, often humming or singing as she did household chores. As a result of her cheerful briskness, she occasionally dropped and broke dishes or other small objects. Instead of expressing annoyance with herself, she would respond straightaway, "Oh, well, it's had its life!" She accepted her small errors as just another normal part of life. Our awareness of our shortcomings doesn't have to reduce our self-respect.

The best way to grow is to be patient and work with the parts of ourselves that were damaged and are flawed. In order to adapt to a dysfunctional family, we father-loss folks learned to deny and repress our feelings. Some of our rough edges we acquired in reaction to our dads. We might not have survived without these tough qualities. Self-love involves constantly facing the truth about ourselves and honoring how we have turned out.

Can we learn to cherish ourselves no matter what we do or don't do? Self-esteem to some extent is quite properly based on our actions. It's fine to appreciate and be proud of what we accomplish. But we can get overly focused on "doing," if we base our self-worth only on our output and success. It's important to feel good about ourselves apart from being productive or even active. It's *who we are*, not just *what we do* that counts.

> **Are we human *doings* or human *beings*?**

The principal key to self-love is to *stop judging ourselves so harshly!* No doubt, we learned how to put ourselves down early in life. We probably have become expert at negative self-talk, regularly berating ourselves with critical statements such as, "I'm not enough... I want too much... I don't have all the answers ... I need to work harder... make more money... be a better parent... have a fuller social life..." And so it goes, on and on.

If we have been used to speaking to ourselves in unfavorable terms, thinking we are inadequate or weak, we are in effect programming our minds to act in the way we describe. Such self-concepts may derive directly from what we heard said about us growing up. They could come from what we deduced about our lack of value based on the way we were treated.

We need to consciously counter these habitual sayings, to deliberately construct an alternative view of ourselves. One of the best ways to do this is to create a series of positive self-descriptions designed to neutralize what we may have spent many years telling ourselves, to balance out the indictments we are accustomed to making.

EXERCISE 35.　AFFIRM YOUR VALUE

You can "accentuate the positive" and practice loving yourself by using affirmations. You've already encountered this technique in another form when you imagined your father encouraging you. Here you directly affirm yourself. These constructive assertions remind you of your capacities and reflect the best in you. You state them in the present rather than future tense to strengthen belief in yourself now. Affirmations directly access your unconscious mind.

Select any of these statements to repeat to yourself silently or aloud, or use them as models to make up your own. Starting out, perhaps two affirmations said three times a day – morning, midday, and bedtime – will suffice. Build up to ten. If you find a declaration no longer touches you, replace it with a different phrase. Keep up indefinitely this habit of reciting affirmations. You'll be glad you did. Reminding yourself of reasons to feel good about yourself makes it easier to maintain a cheerful disposition. These are some of my personal favorites.

I am enough.
I have every reason to be happy.
I love myself and see the good within me.
I am a bright, talented, and creative man/woman.
I am attractive inside and out.
I am an industrious, productive, and competent person.
I have an abundance of friends.
My life brims over with enjoyable activities and interests.
I like my work, and I have a multitude of career options.
I have enough money for security, growth, and pleasure.
I am deeply loved.
I am a precious child of God.
I feel glad to be alive.

Please note that this exercise, like various others, calls for repetition several times a week. Establishing a routine which includes time for affirmations takes a commitment which is not always easy to ask of yourself. However, the minutes that you dedicate to this ongoing process can offset years of mistreatment and neglect you've already experienced.

You may want to put the phrases you choose on your refrigerator or bathroom mirror. Recite them while doing your normal routines, like showering, preparing food, or driving, in order to establish a regular custom. You can accompany a recording you make of them. To use time effectively, I keep a tape recorder in my bathroom. My morning ritual includes playing Jai Josefs' songs on *Loving Your Self* and *Warriors of the Heart* as I shower and put on makeup. I also listen to inspirational cassettes in my car. Those which have worked the best for me I offer on the order form at the back of the book.

Re-creating your internal environment will bring you a more rewarding external life. What happens outside you reflects what's inside. Repeating these positive expressions is helpful in etching new habits in your mind. To actually form different patterns of thought and feeling requires sustained commitment. As with frequent exercise, if you put in the effort, you reap pleasurable results. Keep faith with yourself by constantly affirming your value.

EXERCISE 36.   JUST BE

Many people with father-wounds made a decision as children that they would have to be extraordinary in order to merit their father's love. You may have concluded that your dad didn't love you because you weren't good enough. It is far more likely he failed to show you the affection you wanted because he simply didn't know how to give it freely, rather than that you were unworthy to receive it.

Yet as a result of this youthful misperception, you may still be stuck in the belief that you have to prove you are exceptional in order to be valued. Successful or not, you are likely to pretend to others that you are better than you feel. Once you realize the stress this places on you to create a false facade, you can start to accept that just being your ordinary self is sufficient to be lovable.

It is important to detach from the habit of working so hard to earn recognition, and to let go of continually focusing on gratifying others. Start making it a priority to give yourself space to satisfy your own needs and pleasure yourself.

Allocate an entire day once a month to having fun. Do only what you want. You might read propped up in bed with pillows all around, take a hike, or just look at the clouds. You could spend the day at the shore or in the mountains. Enjoy friends, movies, hobbies, hot air ballooning – whatever gives you pleasure and makes you feel that you're not under pressure to have a predetermined outcome.

In addition, make a point to "just be" at least once each day. You can luxuriate in this state or make it brief, depending on the time you have. Try eating in the open air, going outside merely to look around, listening to music, or watching creatures like cats, birds, or insects.

These "meditative actions" are suggestions of *doing* modes that can help bring you into a *being* state. Treat these not as tasks, but as means to let yourself savor where you are. The instructive motto "Be here now" encourages you to be present and responsive to what's happening each instant.

Quieting yourself in this way opens you to experience moments of inner peace with the Universe. You can pause long enough from your everyday busy-ness to hear a reassuring whisper say, "You're okay. Allow what is to be. You don't have to control everything. Just enjoy yourself."

It is up to you to love yourself fully, merely for being alive. How much you accept yourself *as you are* is a good measure of your level of self-development. Above all, to continue growing, you need to be gentle with yourself, expecting neither flawlessness nor complete freedom from the consequences of father-loss. Be satisfied and pleased with your progress and improvement, knowing that even backsliding is often part of the process of evolution.

You have made tremendous strides toward your transformation. Think how much ground you have covered thus far! You have considered the extent and nature of your dad's effect on you and worked diligently to release your feelings and come to terms with your past. You have learned to validate your inner child and develop self-fathering skills. You have acknowledged the wisdom of your father-wound, re-evaluating its legacy and discovering a larger spiritual perspective from which to view yourself with more understanding. You are allocating more time to fulfill your needs and have reached a point of interior equilibrium. At last you are ready to decide how you want to relate to your father in the present, whether he is dead or alive.

* All the drawings in this book are by father-wound workshop participants. They used their non-dominant hands to get in touch with intense childhood feelings about their dads.

SECTION SEVEN

RECONNECTING WITH YOUR DAD

Using your healing as a foundation, it is finally time to establish a more equitable and rewarding relationship with your father. Understandably, you may feel reluctant or resistant as you consider reconnecting with your dad. You may be apprehensive about how he will react to your being more open with him. You may even feel that being with him in a new way is out of the question. Yet if you are ready to take some emotional risks, facing up to your father can greatly empower you. You can now become a more active participant in defining how the two of you relate.

Approaching your father as an adult gives you experience in speaking up for yourself, setting limits, and showing compassion. These personal skills are vital in achieving intimacy with anyone. Still, a major test of the communication level you've reached is how you deal with your dad.

Although *your* father may have died, he still lives on in your thoughts.

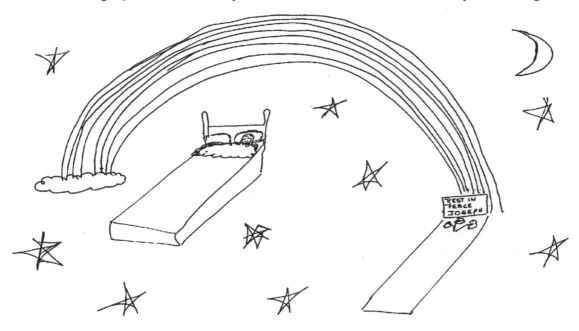

As you review the following discussion about how to evolve relationships with dads who are alive, let yourself feel what it might be like if your father were still living. How did the two of you interact before he passed on? How did you handle his loss?

It may seem paradoxical, but as a mature person, you can consider a whole new range of alternatives in connecting with your dad, *even if he is dead*. These will liberate you from the burden of maintaining your childhood stance toward him or accepting only what others have told you about him. Toward the end of this section you will find specific suggestions for bonding with your deceased father. Reading over these recommendations can also prepare those of you whose fathers are still living for the day when he will no longer be with you.

IF YOUR FATHER IS ALIVE

FINDING THE RIGHT LEVEL OF CONTACT

Having released the hold of the past and stepped into your power, you have three basic options about how involved you want to become with your father. The first and most drastic possibility is to decide to **disconnect from him completely**. The second alternative is to **accept that your relationship may not improve much**. Your challenge is to find a way to make peace with this fact and enjoy your time with him as much as possible. The third and most gratifying prospect is to **build a more genuine friendship with him**. As two adults sharing a common personal history, you can choose to create together a new reality. Of course, he too is free to determine how much participation he wants with you.

> **Relationships require two to say "yes," but only one to say "no."**

Please understand that developing a different relationship with your dad is not critically necessary for you to heal your father-wound. What matters most is that you have developed into someone who is in control of your boundaries. Whatever your association with your dad may become in the future, it will unfold as a conscious choice that *you* make as a grown-up and worthy person, not as the wounded child you were in the past.

Go over all the following material on the three options for connecting with your father, no matter how you may be feeling about him at this moment. For some, none of the described paths will exactly fit your situation. Others may be in transition between alternatives. You can tailor-make your unique solution. In any case, make a deliberate decision to rework your relationship with your dad, on your own terms, based on your newfound understanding and strength.

BREAKING IT OFF

After due consideration, you may conclude that your growth and mental health would be best served by cutting off contact with your father altogether. Sometimes it is too hurtful to associate at all with a dad, especially if he is still abusive, heavily judgmental, or controlling. Replicating old destructive patterns could stifle the precious healing process you are undertaking.

Now that you have fortified your self-esteem, you may find that any communication whatsoever with your father tends to diminish your dignity and natural sense of value. Take stock of your situation and make a determination for yourself alone. If you think this is the only way you can maintain your autonomy as an individual, it is right to make the difficult choice to separate.

This doesn't have to be a lifetime decision. You may make up your mind to disengage from your father for a while and then try again later down the line. You or he may change over time, so allow yourself to be flexible.

As a variation, you might choose to take a hiatus from your father or your family of origin for a short period, perhaps three to six months, to give yourself an opportunity to break away from the powerful pull of prior patterns. You may be used to constantly attempting to take care of your dad's needs or fulfilling his expectations of how you should be. A temporary withdrawal can give you space to solidify changes in yourself, without holding back for fear of offending him or feeling guilty.

My client Ginny recently determined not to go to her folks' home for the holidays. Despite being bored and miserable, she has been spending time with her family merely out of duty. Not wanting to make up an excuse, she simply told them she didn't choose to be with them. She isn't sure how she will feel next year, but she no longer wants dread of disapproval to run her life.

It may take considerable courage to sever from a negative attachment with your father. This action can free you from the unhealthy influence of a toxic environment. To proceed with a clear conscience, be sure that you have first genuinely tried to improve your relationship. If you need help to disconnect, consider seeking support from a friend, group, or professional.

Even though you may believe you need to break off with your father now, keep reading. You could decide in the future that reestablishing some limited contact with him is worth the risk. In that case, the following sections offer you valuable suggestions about how to reconnect with your dad.

ACCEPTING THE RELATIONSHIP AS IT IS

If your father is not receptive to a warm emotional bond, despite your desire to grow closer, it is important for you to accept him where he is. Possibly no one can break through his distance barrier. Once you have genuinely tried to be more open with him, and he still doesn't respond, at least you know that you've done the most you could. You may have to reconcile yourself to seeing him without great depths of sharing.

A workshop member described her disappointment at the results of her efforts to involve her father more in her life. "I approached my dad by phone. I asked him to come to my wedding, but he couldn't. He had to work. I also visited him for dinner at his house in Florida and introduced him to my fiancé two years ago. My visits and conversations with him are always pleasant, but superficial. We talk about what we're doing, about everyone in the family. But we never discuss feelings."

You should guard, however, against settling too easily for just making the best of it. Your dad's unwillingness to communicate meaningfully could also be a reflection of your fear of disclosing yourself to him. Before you write him off as unable to confront his sensitive issues, be sure *you* aren't avoiding being straight about yours. Your father's inability to be open doesn't have to stop your growth process. In fact, you can note the effects on his life of evading intimacy, probably with other people as well as you. Learn from his example not to do the same.

Your father's limited interaction with you reflects his own personal inhibitions, not necessarily yours. As a former client of mine wrote me, "My relationship with my dad is still lousy, but I'm less bothered by it." You are born with just one natural father. If you can adjust your expectations and let him relate to you in his style, being with him can be satisfying.

There may be many simple ways you can spend more time together, such as taking walks, doing projects around the house, or going to the movies. Enjoy what is possible. Moderating your desires is less frustrating than trying to make him over.

MOVING TOWARD A CLOSER CONNECTION

The third and most preferable choice is to move toward greater friendship and sharing with your father. The man who was unable to provide what you wanted when you were a child may now be a bit older and wiser and is perhaps ready to give more concern and time to you. Throughout the process of reconnecting with your dad, let your heart be your guide.

A seminar participant wrote the following story about how her father changed as he aged. "My dad and I have a good relationship today, which has evolved over the past 12 years since he stopped drinking. I've recently come back from a visit with my parents in the Midwest. Dad had just had a hip replacement; he is 82 now. I talked to him a lot and asked questions about his life, childhood, his mom and dad. He blossomed. He opened up and talked so much. I grew a lot in my understanding of both him and mom. He took me all over town and showed me hills he used to sleigh ride down and the park where he and mom used to 'spoon.'

"It was so bittersweet, so touching – sharing with this now frail, sweet old man, who once scared the B-Jesus out of me. I'll always remember this visit. I cried every night in bed and wrote in my journal, so I'd capture the memories and feelings. There's still much distance between us, a sense of strangers just becoming friends. I think he was literally unconscious throughout much of my childhood."

You are the one to begin reaching out to your father. The relationship can improve, but you must be willing to take the risk of making yourself vulnerable. Your greater compassion for your dad's pain and sadness can create a clearing between you. Be open to meeting him more than half way. You have the chance to pay him back for however much care-giving he contributed to you earlier.

Building a warmer friendship with your father is an excellent investment of your energy. If you feel there is even a remote chance that the two of you might be able to start over, I urge you to make the effort. The rewards will enrich most areas of your life. Of course, many complex remembrances and feelings are bound to emerge. Go slowly. There is no hurry. Extend yourself at a safe and comfortable pace.

Initiating the Change

Any relationship with your father must be based on accepting him *the way he is now.* You can hardly expect him to spontaneously change, especially as he grows older. Nonetheless, he may want to connect with his grown children in a new manner but not know how.

The best means for you to strengthen your tie with your father is to *change the way you treat him.* Your willingness to work on yourself has put you in a better position to initiate a shift in how the two of you interact. Perhaps in the past, you've been overreactive or oversensitive to your dad. It may no longer be necessary to defend yourself against him. Consciously altering the way you act toward him could have a remarkably positive effect on his attitude.

Be careful not to set yourself up for disappointment, hoping for an unrealistic degree of connection with him. On the other hand, don't assume that there is a limit to the depth of bonding that might develop between you.

A workshop member described the beginnings of an open exchange with his father. "I stayed at my dad's house last Christmas, and late one night after his second wife went to bed, we began to talk about what it was like living with mom. He said she would nag him sometimes from the moment he walked in the door or immediately tell him what the kids did wrong and how he should punish them. He told me he had tried his best not to argue with her in front of us children.

"We spoke for almost two hours about how it was for each of us. When we finished, I told him how much it meant to me for him to share with me. He said he liked it too, because no one else had ever talked to him like that. That made me feel very good. I had always seen Dad as unapproachable on sensitive issues. That night, he shared some things he had held in for a long time."

Establishing an Equal Footing

One key to achieving a new level of relationship with your father is to approach him as a peer – adult to adult. In place of being passive or complaining, you can claim your power. Interchanges between you can become more forthright. For greater balance, consider calling him by his first name.

Let him know that you care about improving communications with him. Connecting with your father more genuinely will require you to talk together frankly. Each of you has your own truth to tell. If you want him to listen to your point of view, then you need to be receptive to hearing his. Acknowledge his pain, in the same way that you would like him to see yours.

Make certain to treat current problems differently from past ones. No matter what level of closeness you achieve, don't let your dad get away with dysfunctional behavior. Set boundaries with him. You don't have to play the child or be demeaned when you're with him. Explain directly how his behavior makes you feel toward him. Sometimes the most affirming action you can take is to state forcefully, "Dad, when you tell me what to do, I feel angry and resentful toward you. I need you to listen to me without giving me advice."

If your father has been accustomed to being intrusive or domineering, he may not even know that he is hurting you. Be clear about what you'd like and what disturbs you. If he oversteps the line you have drawn, you can get up and leave. In the long run, asserting what's appropriate for you will be what's best for your dad as well.

Your internal releasing work has resolved many past injuries. The more you let go of your residual feelings, the more present you can be with your dad. If you find you can't bring up touchy subjects without justifying yourself or making him wrong, stop for the time being. To be able to speak to your dad without resentment, consider going back over the exercises that encourage you to express and let go of your pain.

Clearing Out the Past

You may feel the need to clear the air by telling your dad about your painful feelings when you were growing up. Sharing your sadness without blaming him or putting him on the defensive makes a more authentic relationship possible. The idea is to voice what has been hurtful between you so you can move on. Be very cautious in talking to him about past abuse, unless you believe he is open to hearing you. If he doesn't acknowledge his complicity, articulating your pain may open the door for still further assaults.

Be sure to prepare your dad for engaging in such a serious discussion. Knowing what issues you want to bring up gives him time to get used to the idea. You might open the conversation with your father in this manner:

"Dad, I want to be closer to you. I have some feelings that are difficult for me to share with you, but I'm afraid I'll feel more distant from you if I don't get them out. I also fear I might hurt your feelings, because you matter so much to me. I don't intend to attack you. We may have some differences to work out, but you are an important part of my life. I really would like you to know that I love you and care about you. Are you willing to hear me and talk with me, Dad?"

Your father may not be receptive to your overtures. He may remain critical or manipulative. He may claim he does not remember key events. Selective recall could block out what doesn't fit his self-image or his idea of your harmonious family. His not recollecting does not invalidate what you believe to be true.

If your father doesn't respond well, thank him for listening, and tell him you might ask to speak to him again at some other time. You must respect your dad's right to decline this type of interaction. Then you'll have to go within to resolve the frustration of his refusing to be vulnerable with you. You might write a letter you don't intend to send, expressing your pain to him. You can read it to others who are more empathic. Not every attempt at sharing will be successful, but you will have done your part.

A client of mine related the following story about meeting her dad for the first time in her life. For many years, he had even denied fathering her. "I went to see my father one and a half years ago. He had cancer of the larynx and could not speak. But he was able to listen to me. I told him how I had felt about being abandoned. He seemed present and to hear me. I insisted he respond to me in writing, but his answers were useless. He was unable to identify why he had abandoned me, or how he felt."

This woman did not get the satisfaction from her dad that she had hoped for. She learned that he was so emotionally shut down that he was unable to meet her needs. Now she can let go of her lingering illusions regarding him and turn instead to the tangible satisfactions that are available to her, with her husband, friends, and in her career.

Should your dad be ready to listen, tell him about the times you were wounded and disappointed by him when you were growing up. Be specific about his behavior. Use the simple formula of "When you…, I felt…" For example, say, "When you hit me across the face after I broke that vase, I felt scared, guilty, and angry." Strong feelings, a shaky voice, or tears may overtake you when you talk to your father. It's good for him to see your pain.

In general, express your hurt rather than your anger. Sustained confrontation rarely works well in building bridges. If you complain about how badly he treated you, your father may become resentful and resistant. If you make him wrong, he'll prove he's right. Attack him, and he'll retaliate. Then both of you are likely to get upset, and the result will work against you. Let him know that you care about his feelings. Refrain from lecturing, browbeating, or trying to make him feel guilty. The main reason for telling the truth is to put the past behind you.

On the other hand, sometimes the only authentic way you can communicate is to express your rage, no matter the reaction. Because your feelings are so intense, you have no hope of peace without telling your dad how angry you are with him. Some people have reported breakthroughs using this confrontive approach. Their fathers eventually got the message and cared enough to work it out with their children. But this course is risky. In other cases, when sons or daughters have voiced their strong emotions, the result has been bitter feelings. Being forceful may indeed be the only way to penetrate your father's settled attitudes. He might not respect you for being accommodating or pleading for his attention.

Be open to your dad's response when you share your perceptions about your former or current wounds. He may regret his behavior and be relieved to talk about his feelings regarding old incidents. A friend asked her father to read an article of mine on the consequences of inadequate fathering. Its point of view was unfamiliar, and the information hit him hard. Feeling remorseful, he told her, "I'm afraid that I wasn't a very good dad." She shared honestly with him the times when she felt hurt, scared, and mad because of him. She also stated her appreciation for his good qualities and the many occasions when he gave her support. He apologized for having caused her pain. He gained a more balanced view of his strengths and weaknesses as a father. By the end of their talk, they had never felt so close.

Pay careful attention to what your dad says and how he says it. If you stay relaxed, you will hear him better. Showing warmth, asking thoughtful questions, and appreciating his feelings without judgment will offer your father a safety zone that may enable him to talk to you openly. If you sense yourself overreacting, slow down and breathe deeply. If what you hear is confusing, ask for clarification. Listen for the feelings underneath his words.

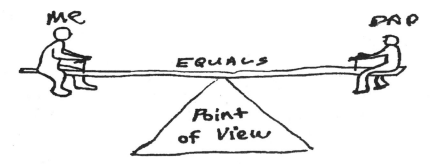

As much as you can, see his point of view. Remember that walking in your dad's shoes does not mean giving up your own path. Explain your perspective to him without wanting or needing his approval. It takes maturity to realize that your father has his own version of reality, especially if it differs from yours. Your goal is not to change his mind, rather to share each of your feelings at a deeper level.

The calmer you are as you reveal yourself, the less likely your father will be to argue or impose his opinions on you. But if he reacts in criticism or hostility, this suggests that he is not yet ready to deal with his actions and history. Stay connected with your own feelings, without taking on your dad's denial, hurt, or rage. Maintaining your center will keep you from feeling guilty or depressed.

In order to make peace with your dad, you also need to be willing to admit your contribution to your mutual problems. Are there errors you made you can acknowledge to him? Were you a handful growing up? Have you been so enraged at him that you tried to wound him or shut him out of your heart? Having found the strength to own up to your part in his hurt, apologizing to your father for your past deeds could open the flow of positive feelings between you.

Starting Over

After you have both had an opportunity to talk about your injuries from the past, tell your dad what you need and want from him now. Do you know what that is? For some, communicating feelings is enough. Others would like their fathers to be more involved in their affairs, from listening to what's happening to them at work to seeing the grandchildren more often. You can request anything, but be careful not to set yourself up for disappointment by going after more than your dad is capable of giving. This reconnection may be new to both of you, so proceed judiciously.

Tell your dad that he is special to you. Let him know that you accept him, that you enjoy being with him. Make him understand that you cherish him and want him in your life. Permit him to see what is in your heart. Regardless of what happens when you reach out to your dad, know that deep down he loves you. Even if he doesn't express his affection well, concealed under his protective armor is caring for his child. No longer needing him to fill your emptiness will take the pressure off your dad. If you ask without demanding, perhaps he will give you the response you want.

As a boy, my friend Joe got attention from his alcoholic dad only by performing well in athletics. When he quit the swimming team at thirteen, his father washed his hands of him, barely speaking to him from then on. At twenty-five, Joe finally went to his dad and said, "Let's be friends, Dad. All I ever wanted was to be your friend." Joe's father slowly nodded and agreed.

Then the son risked saying, "You never tell me you love me." Joe's dad, who is in a helping profession, seemed flustered. He responded, "I love everybody." The young man countered, "I need you to tell *me*." Now his father often remembers to put his love for his son into words.

EXERCISE 37. STRATEGIES TO CONNECT WITH YOUR DAD

It is often difficult knowing how to begin a new relationship with your father. Avoid preset expectations of what will happen. You're seeing what is possible between you. It doesn't have to work out a certain way. He may not be accustomed to answering personal questions or spending quality time with you. Be patient, go little by little, and give him space to come around. Here are a number of suggestions. Try at least two.

- **Give your dad a hug the next time you see him.**

The hug could initially be mechanical, but after a while the fondness that is buried underneath will start to come through. If you and your dad already hug each other, you can embrace him with more feeling than usual. He may be uncomfortable at first, but don't give up. If you're persistent, he is likely to respond. Don't be shy with him. *Be the one who initiates.* Rub his shoulders or take his hand on a walk. Give him unexpected notes and gifts. If you feel warmly toward him, how about making a point of saying so? At the end of a visit or phone conversation, you can simply say, "I love you, Dad."

- **Take your father out to lunch on a regular basis.**

Commonly, when an adult child calls his or her folks, dad answers by saying, "Hi. How are you? I'll get your mother." He's used to letting his wife maintain family connections. Say directly, "Dad, I want to talk to *you*." If you live nearby, invite him out for lunch periodically. This could cause problems for your mother, step-mother, or siblings, who customarily run interference for him or primarily interact with you. Be clear that you want to be alone with your father. If the two of you can talk on a personal level, that's great. If not, merely sharing the experience is important.

- **Spend a few days away on a mini-vacation with just your dad.**

Arrange a trip and plan activities that both of you will enjoy. Find out more about your father by being with him apart from work and family. You and he can embark on some adventures. If your budget doesn't allow you to travel, make a point to schedule some fun activities you can do together. Leave plenty of time to just sit around and get to know each other.

After taking my father-loss workshop, Marge approached her father in a new way. Instead of asking him if he'd like to   visit her in California, she said, "Dad, I'm sending you a plane ticket. When do you want to come?" After they arranged a date, she went on to say, "I don't recall knowing much about your background when I was a kid. Do you think you could talk to me about your earlier life?" Her father responded, "I've got a bunch of pictures. I'll bring them out." She was pleased at the lack of the usual tension between them. She had not seen her seventy-one year old dad for four years. He is crippled with bursitis and arthritis. She says she wants "to get right with the man before he dies."

- **Peruse old photographs of you and your dad.**

Seeing how much your father treasured you as a child can help you feel more connected to him today. Tony, a workshop participant, reported, "I looked at pictures from way back when I was a baby.

My dad was holding me, and he seemed like he was having a good time. It made me realize my father really did love me. He had a lot of pride in his face in those photos, and it makes me feel more forgiving. Things weren't great after a few years, but in those beginning days he must have loved me a lot."

- **Sit down with your father, possibly with a tape recorder, and get his version of the family history.**

Ask for information you'd really like to know. Urge him on by saying, "What I want to find out is... Tell me more about... I'm especially curious regarding..." Take an active interest. Your dad may feel that no one cares about his stories from the past. This is a real gift you can bestow on him which provides both of you a good way to connect.

Not long before his father died, a friend of mine spent a great deal of time with him, asking questions, taping his whole biography. He edited the transcripts into a family book, illustrating the narrative with vintage snapshots. My friend is very glad that the old man got to relate his stories and that there is now such a detailed keepsake to remind him of his dad.

- **Create a videotape about your father's life as a present to him.**

Record a personal interview with your dad, then combine it with early photos, old home movies, and more recent video clips. In the process, you will get to know him much better. Such tapes are ways you can remember the best of your heritage, and these memoirs will become increasingly valuable to you as the years pass.

Reconnecting with your father can be a major step in your healing process. At least one of these means will probably provide an opportunity to experience more closeness with your dad. Few people can resist a determined effort to give them love. On the other hand, your father may remain closed. In that case, you still benefit from having risked. You faced your fears by moving toward him. Give yourself credit for endeavoring to establish more meaningful ties with your dad.

EXERCISE 38.   EXCHANGE REQUESTS WITH YOUR DAD

If your initial attempts to reach out to your father yield good results, you may be ready for a still better interaction. Perhaps neither of you has directly communicated what would make you more comfortable with the other. This exercise can improve your relationship by helping the two of you specify what each wants.

One way to let your father know that you are interested in deepening your connection is to describe three favors you would like from him. Ask him to choose the one that he is most willing to do, but let him know that he need not respond immediately, rather he should take twenty-four hours to consider them.

Propose that during this period he also think of three actions he would like you to take which he believes would make your relations work better. Promise in turn to do what you can to fulfill at least one of his wishes. The two sets of requests can increase your mutual understanding by showing each of you what's important to the other person.

Get clear on something you'd like to give your dad, even if he doesn't make a request. By knowing ahead of time what you want from him and what you are willing to offer, you set the tone for a win-win encounter.

Keep it simple. Like everyone, fathers relish most of all acknowledgment and acceptance, which create the basis for a growing companionship. Listen to his concerns. Give feedback. Make eye contact. Providing attention and respect conveys your love for your dad.

Deepening Your Experience

Search within and write out answers to the following questions in your journal.

- Have I truly tried to improve my relationship with my father?
- What type of connection do I want with him?
- What am I willing to do to have this happen?
- Are there any amends I need to make to him?

Create a collage depicting how you would like to interact with your dad. For example, cut out pictures from magazines of two people talking over coffee, walking, gardening, or playing chess together.

IF YOUR FATHER IS DEAD

"Death ends a life, but not a relationship," says a line from Robert Anderson's play, *I Never Sang For My Father*. One psychological researcher told me she found that young female students who had lost a father felt a great desire to know how to make an on-going connection to their past. They would say to her, "My dad has not been in my life for a number of years, yet he is such a part of me. How can I deal with my memories of him so they enhance my sense of my own history and make-up?"

You too may want to make a deeper bond with your deceased father, to incorporate him more fully into your daily life. Some of you could have unfinished business with a dad who passed away suddenly or when you were very young. It is natural to want to feel the presence of a father who is no longer with you in person. Despite his being dead, you can still identify with your dad and communicate with him.

EXERCISE 39.   ENCOUNTER YOUR DECEASED DAD

You can connect with your deceased father emotionally and spiritually when you feel the need. What follows are ways that might help you link with him. Some of these suggestions presuppose life after death, which may not fit within your belief system. Use what feels right for you.

• **Talk to your dad out loud or just internally.**

You can ask for his counsel as you go through your day. Say what's in your heart, such as, "Dad, do you see my problem here? I'd like a suggestion as to what to do now. I believe you care. I know you're with me." He will respond, if you can learn to quiet yourself enough to hear his answers. To make yourself more receptive, relax your chest and stomach. Breathe deeply and wait to see what thoughts materialize in your mind.

• **Write to your father in journal form.**

Make entries like this one: "Dear Dad, let me tell you what happened today…" Then three days later, you note: "Dear Dad, this is what I went through this afternoon…" Your personal journal becomes a series of letters to your father.

• **Collect physical objects that belonged to your dad.**

You can carry around something of his or keep it in your house to remind you of your association with him. Some families in which the father is gone treat him as though he never existed. The adults don't mention him and subtly discourage the children from asking questions about him. For example, one woman's dad died in the Korean War when she was a toddler. Her mother never spoke of him. Then when the daughter was in her twenties, her mom gave her the father's leather flight jacket with all its colorful insignia. She proudly wore her dad's coat, and people often asked her about it. Telling his story activated feelings she had long denied. This jacket revived her link with her father and started the process of healing her loss.

• **Search out and meet with your father's relatives and friends.**

Try to reconstruct a realistic picture of who your dad was. Read a novel or history book set during the period he was growing up. You might travel to the place he was born to better understand his roots and yours. Ask questions about him and gather stories. Talking with several people who knew him can give you different perspectives on what he was like.

• **Make a pilgrimage to your father's burial site.**

You can speak to his spirit, acknowledging what he meant to you. This is a very good way to feel in touch with him and express what

you need to say. If his grave is not readily accessible, go to where his ashes were scattered, to a shoreline, or to an isolated natural setting. Read out loud the letter to him that you wrote in an earlier exercise. Then burn it. Sit there for at least an hour and just be with your thoughts and feelings. You help release the pain of his loss through saying farewell.

A young woman in one of my classes figured out her own version of this process. "My dad is cremated, and his ashes are placed way up in a mausoleum. I can't see myself going to that spot to talk to my dad. I know – the golf course! My dad loved the fairways. I could go when no one else is around and speak to and connect with him there."

• Ask your father to make contact with you in dreams.

Before you go to sleep, request that your dad visit you during the night. I have heard many stories about fathers appearing in this manner. After her dad passed away, class member Jodi dreamed that he came to her and said, "I'm just like I was before I died. I'm simply not there where you are. I'm not on the same plane with you." Jodi's experience was a confirmation to her that there is a spirit that lives on after death. Her dad was not really lost. He merely wasn't immediately available to her in his body anymore.

Communicating with your deceased father in the ways I have suggested is more than a psychological strategy. From a metaphysical point of view, your dad still exists in another dimension, and you can connect to him. I make my father part of my spiritual life every day by asking for his help and guidance. Wherever he is, I believe he cares what happens to me and has the ability to help me.

HEALING AS A LIFELONG THEME

Recovering from any wound takes time. Years from now, you may find yourself grappling with some remnant of your father-loss that you thought you had long since overcome. Yet you discover you still have more to clear. Such are the recurring themes in the song of healing.

At this point, you have gone through the entire process for repairing your father-wound. Nonetheless, you might benefit from reviewing and redoing certain exercises and even whole sections. Mourning and letting go are especially important. Because family histories are so deep-reaching and complex, you may spend years working through to full-scale emotional release.

EXERCISE 40.   ACKNOWLEDGE YOUR GROWTH

Now it's time to take a few steps back from doing individual practices to survey the big picture of your personal growth. Though this review will be rather lengthy and detailed, it is one of the most valuable and rewarding processes in the book. This is your opportunity to see how you've integrated the various exercises to make the seven-step recovery plan work for you. You also get to acknowledge and reinforce all the headway you have made.

For this re-examination, you go back through the book, section by section, repeating three basic steps. In Step One, you look at which exercises were particularly effective and evocative for you. Step Two offers you a well-deserved opportunity to pat yourself on the back for the many successes you have achieved. Step Three asks you to identify those portions of the recovery process that still feel incomplete. You can assess more closely what work remains for you to do.

Assemble all the various exercise aids you have generated since you began working through this guidebook. These will include your journal, audio tapes, letters, drawings, collages, family photos, mementoes, even your teddy bear. As you go along, be ready to consult the Table of Contents and the "Seven Steps to Healing" segment in the Introduction. Set aside space in your journal to write out responses to a series of questions. Moving from Section One through Seven, finish all three steps for each section before proceeding to the next.

Allow yourself plenty of time to complete this reappraisal. Your replies to each question may be very brief, or you may find yourself writing many paragraphs. There is no right length. Some answers may not come to you in one sitting, instead emerging unexpectedly, while you are driving, working, or dreaming. This careful self-examination will evoke new realizations, and writing them down will lock in their significance for you.

Retracing all this material may seem like a daunting task. It will take longer than most of the other exercises have. Yet if you can rise to the challenge, this reconsideration offers you a wonderful opportunity to give yourself a check-up, a thorough scrutiny of where you stand now in relation to your father-wound.

Step 1. Review your responses to the exercises.

The emphasis at this point is on your favorable reactions. This step encourages you to reflect on your experience of the processes in each section as a set, so you can more fully grasp how they work together. It's like walking around a whole floor to see the design of a house, rather than staying inside one room. Creating a composite view encourages depth perception, reinforces the insights you have already had, and helps you see more clearly what you have gained.

Note that the same exercise may be the answer to more than one of the following questions. For example, a particular process might be your favorite and be the one that was most important for you as well. Ask yourself:

• **Which exercise did I like the best? What did I like about it?**

• **Which process produced the most powerful effect on me? Why do I think it made so much of an impact?**

• **From which exercise did I learn the most? What did it teach me about myself that I didn't know before?**

In writing about Section Four, "Healing the Child Within," one workshop member responded to these questions in this way. "I liked the 'Teddy Bear' exercise the best because it was easy and fun for me. I got my old teddy out of the attic. Now he reads with me in bed, and his company soothes me. 'Your Daddy Loves You' affected me the most. I was so touched and comforted to hear loving words from a daddy. I really choked up reading those phrases out loud.

I learned most from 'Touches and Hugs.' I like to think I am open and loving, so I was surprised how hard it was at first to be physically affectionate with my friends. When put to the test, I found myself holding back, feeling scared even when I wanted to give hugs. Once I realized this, I persisted in taking the risk. Now, it's one of the delights of my life to give and receive hugs. I even tell people I *collect* hugs to encourage them to give me one."

Step 2. Applaud your successes.

This is an occasion to acknowledge yourself for all the time and effort you have devoted to your transformation. You have good reason to be proud. You have digested a tremendous amount of challenging material. Just as in viewing the "before and after" photos of someone who has lost a great deal of weight, you can remind yourself where you started and how much territory you've covered.

Your family may have erroneously trained you to discount your achievements by telling you not to brag or be self-centered. But you deserve to sit back and contemplate your evolution with great satisfaction. Take this opportunity to appreciate the specifics of your accomplishment.

Each stage in the healing process has led you to a new plateau of satisfaction. Advance on one level has made growth in the next possible. Identifying the observable life changes that have happened for you will enable you to gauge just how much you have evolved. Remember that you are after progress, not perfection. Concerning each section, ask yourself:

- **To what degree have I released stuck feelings, healed old wounds, and expanded as an individual?**

- **In what distinct ways do I now feel better about myself and treat myself with more kindness and respect?**

- **What actions and attitudes have I altered? How has my daily experience improved?**

The same workshop member wrote, "With respect to 'Healing the Child Within,' I feel differently about myself. I am less self-critical now and more accepting that I'm doing the best I can. I'm aware that I really do have a baby and little child inside of me who require attention. Every day I enjoy thinking about what they need from me. I can actually see myself as this little girl about five years old who is sad and lonely. Then I imagine my adult self being comforting and playful with her, and she becomes happy and energetic."

Step 3. Take a deep and honest look at those areas of your life where you need to do more work.

This is another chance to sort through your unresolved father-loss issues. The more specific you can be about what still needs attention, the more manageable the task will become. Old hurts and dysfunctional behaviors don't just go away by themselves. Continuing to risk the sometimes difficult, fearful, and gut-wrenching labor of healing leads to relief, empowerment, and joy. You can extend still further whatever peace, understanding, and maturity you have already gained.

Your reactions to each of the various processes combine together to form a kind of fill-in-the-dot drawing, outlining a picture of yourself. How you carried them all out tells a great deal about your traits and preferences. You may or may not have liked getting into your emotions, doing visualizations, researching into your background, or changing how you relate to others.

Examining whether you welcomed or avoided certain exercises can reveal patterns from the past that you may still be repeating now. For example, you may notice that you resisted "Proclaim Your Power," where you were asked to support your inner child in demanding justice from your father. This could indicate that you generally have difficulty in openly asserting your needs in standing up for what you want. You may have had trouble with "The Process of Forgiving." In thinking about why, you may realize that you have a tendency to blame others for your problems rather than taking personal responsibility for how you handled difficult situations. When you identify such characteristic responses, you understand yourself better and can guard against letting these attitudes dominate your behavior.

As you focus in on your unfinished business, consider what further steps you might take to gain resolution for yourself. You can redo some exercises or journal extensively on a given topic. You might be able to apply the tools from one process to assist you in another sphere. For instance, if you find you can't forgive your father, discuss the situation with your Witness and see whether s/he can suggest new approaches. You might enlist the aid of a friend, join a support group, attend a pertinent workshop, or get into counseling. Section by section, probe yourself closely as follows:

- **Which exercise(s) didn't I do? As I look back, did I not undertake them simply because they didn't relate to my situation, or did I put them off because they seemed too complicated or difficult? Am I open to giving any of them a try in the next few weeks?**

- **Which processes did I merely confront half-heartedly? What can I learn about myself by fully exploring the reasons I skimmed them? Am I now willing to redo them with more application?**

- **Could I gain from repeating any of the exercises, even those from which I have already profited?**

- **Would I benefit from asking for help from others to further my growth in certain areas?**

Completing her overview of Section Four, this lady wrote, "I didn't do the 'Kudos' one. I was criticized so much when I was younger that it is hard for me to acknowledge – let alone write down – good comments others say to me. I can see now how crucial it is that I make that list of compliments and keep adding to it.

Resisting hugging and touching for so long plus not writing kudos add up to me not allowing myself very much pleasure. My dad was a workaholic, and I see that I'm following the same pattern that I disliked in him: lots of work and very little fun. I resolve to take more time off for enjoyable activities like skiing and dancing. I'll enlist my best friend's help by asking her to let me know when she sees that I'm not responding positively to compliments people give me. "

Be sure to congratulate yourself for your progress. Add in some laughter, hugs, and "Hoorays." Consider how deeply many of these exercises touched you and how much your responses to them tell you about yourself. As you note what else you need to do, be gentle with yourself, knowing that the path to wholeness takes time and work.

You've now completed the seven steps of healing the father-wound. When you consider how your father left, neglected, or mistreated you, your stomach doesn't churn as often nor your heart ache so much. You may remember the rejecting or cruel actions he took toward you, but with less inner charge.

You achieve clarity in the present when you accept what happened in the past. There is no longer an attempt to change your dad or the situation. He was who he had to be. You can now tell yourself, "I am free to go on from here and make my life wonderful. I can be however I want." Reaching this point means that you finally have let go. Instead of wishing for what could have been, you are creating what can be.

Now you're ready to put together everything you've learned, so you can more fully enjoy your relationships. Your adult friendships may have suffered due to painful damage and unmet needs from your past. Recovery prepares the ground for you to make healthier connections.

SECTION EIGHT

BUILDING SATISFYING RELATIONSHIPS

At last we are prepared to turn our attention toward relationships with individuals in our lives besides our dads, which is where father-loss most significantly impacts us. Grappling with our father-wound has made us less emotionally needy. Having laid a new inner foundation, we can feel confident enough to open ourselves to a greater degree of intimacy.

Relationships can be terribly painful. I remember my suffering when a romance ended or there was no man in my life. While I was with a partner, I desperately wanted to feel secure. In order to please him, I concentrated on fulfilling his needs and downplayed my own. Believing he adored me produced a temporary relief from feeling alone and empty. Without my realizing it, my past controlled me. I wanted my partner to give me the unconditional love my father could not provide. I was looking for acceptance outside of myself, not knowing how to find it from within.

Once we understand the nature of our father-wound, we can see how we are repeating old patterns with friends and loved ones. The dynamics of relationships can actually help us carry on the healing process. We may use our reactions to our intimates to get in touch with unresolved areas of father-loss. Even our upsets can provide a means to access deep-seated disabling belief systems.

Personal bonds facilitate recovery in many ways. When we express pain about the past to our companions, we have the chance to acknowledge and quiet

our fear of abandonment. We nurture our inner child by admitting our needs. We empower ourselves by setting boundaries against mistreatment and allocating time for pleasure. Opening up emotionally to a few people that we trust is vital for our growth. One of the great gifts that close connections bestow is the opportunity to rework our basic sense of self.

FATHER SUBSTITUTES

When we were children, many of us went to the father well, only to find it dry. No one can replace the daddy we wanted. However, as adults, we can discover men who will act as *mentors* for us. Our self-esteem increases when father substitutes show an interest in us and model strength and warmth.

Studies have shown that despite growing up in difficult circumstances, such as poverty, abuse, or abandonment, some people manage to live happy, productive lives. Yet others from similar backgrounds end up emotionally or physically crippled, in jail, or dead prematurely. One common factor for those who succeed is having someone outside the family, such as a teacher, scoutmaster, or neighbor take an active interest in them as youngsters.

My friend John is grateful for the positive impact that surrogate fathers have had on his life. The first was his step-father, who adopted him and gave him his name. Later, he progressed under a high school coach, and finally as a grown man encountered a spiritual teacher who inspired him. These men came into John's life when he needed them most.

There are many types of paternal substitutes. One special category is an "adopted father." Sometimes there is such a strong a link between you and an older man that he invites you to think of him as your dad. When I was in my twenties, I was fortunate to be with one such person for a brief time. On a flight to Brazil, I met a kindly older couple from Venezuela. We explored Rio de Janiero together during the days and met for dinner in the evenings.

Then they invited me to spend time with them in their home in Caracas. After a few days there, Alberto and Maria asked me to call them "Mama and Papa." One afternoon strolling through the shopping district, Papa wanted to buy me a pink hat we saw in a store window. I was very touched by his expression of caring, yet refused the gift because I was so uncomfortable accepting a present from a "dad." As my plane took off, tears of loss streamed down my cheeks. At that moment, I sensed how much I had missed growing up without a father.

EXERCISE 41. FATHER SUBSTITUTES FROM THE PAST

Father figures have probably touched you at various points. As a small child, in grade school, during adolescence, or as an adult, a substitute dad may have supplied a healing, supportive interaction.

Take a walk through your life. Use a "father substitute scanner" while you watch yourself grow up. Do you have fond memories as a young child of a favorite uncle, an older brother, or a friendly neighbor? Do your school age years bring back images of a responsive teacher, coach, or counselor? Sift through the college professors, military officers, bosses, business associates, and service professionals you've known.

Be aware of warmhearted or grateful feelings you have toward these individuals. Did they take a special interest in your education or career? Maybe someone was tough on you when you needed discipline or direction. Often people affect us deeply, without their even knowing it. Acknowledge the kind of fathering you received from these men who positively impacted you.

Now write down their names. Allow yourself to recall the pleasure of the connection with each person who was committed or caring toward you. Think of conversations or activities that were significant to you, whether the contribution was short-term or extensive. Next to every name, describe what this person gave you as a "dad."

If possible, you might consider contacting each of these stand-in dads to say hello and to tell him that you recognize and value what he provided you. Expressing your gratitude confirms the gift you received. This reaching out can complete a circle of attention and concern that began years earlier.

Sarah, a single mother in her thirties, related to me how a close acquaintance of the family helped replace her own father, who deserted home when she was a little girl. "My mother had an older male friend who was just like a dad to me. He spent the holidays with us and came over frequently on Sundays," she explained. Even after her mom died, Sarah maintained a close relationship with him. He "fathered" her and "grandfathered" her children. "We were all winners," she says.

PRESENT–DAY FATHER FIGURES

In the past, we tried *unconsciously* to find the fathering we needed. This search brought havoc to some of our associations, as we unknowingly attempted to get lovers, bosses, or friends to act as substitute dads. Now we can *consciously* activate this process. Finding men who would make good stand-in fathers is not an essential component to healing the father-wound, but it can be a delightful and rewarding experience. Often potential mentors are already part of our lives. We may simply need to open ourselves to the opportunities available with the people around us.

Father substitutes need not even know that we are giving them this status. Indeed, we may only see these men occasionally or for just one encounter, such as consulting with a clergyman who helps us resolve a crisis. These emotionally touching interchanges help shift our perceptions of ourselves. Paternal surrogates reinforce our growing sense that we are valuable and deserve recognition and support. When they believe in us and urge us to go after our goals, we learn to be more accepting and encouraging toward ourselves. It is especially gratifying when substitute dads give us reinforcement we were deprived of as we were growing up.

Mentors provide *men* the experience of deep male bonding. It is healing for a fellow who lacked good fathering, when another man in a position to help takes the time to advise him. Jason, a thirty-year old friend of mine, spends a lot of time at his girlfriend's parents' house. Her dad has spent many hours showing Jason how to install and fix things around the house. The young man's own father never taught him these practical skills. More than that, a warm bond has developed that my friend didn't experience with his own dad.

For *women*, looking to our mates to be second fathers puts too much weight, and the wrong kind of demand, on intimate companionships. At times, concerned spouses offer appropriate father-like comforting. Yet frequently casting our lovers in a paternal role gives too much of our power away to them. A romantic union calls for equity and mutual exchange between partners. In contrast, the father-daughter connection is inherently unbalanced, dissimilar, and unequal. If we want good and unencumbered love relationships, it's better to find our father fill-ins somewhere else.

Seeking father substitutes is often more complicated for women than men. "Proceed with caution" is good advice here. Male associates who are potential counselors can misperceive a lady's interest in them as being sexually oriented. Often a female has only been conditioned to befriend men through flirting, so she may inadvertently send the wrong signals. Few men and women are familiar with how to maintain Platonic friendships. While establishing a pleasant person-to-person tone, women can keep connections non-romantic by setting clear boundaries against unwelcome advances and by not "leaking" sexual energy.

CARING PROFESSIONALS

One way to enhance your life is to turn some of the professionals you visit into father substitutes. With careful selection, you can find persons who provide you with competent service and also care about you as an individual. I consult a mix of men and women specialists: a doctor, dentist, lawyer, accountant, and business adviser. I deal exclusively with those who, in addition to being proficient, seem to genuinely enjoy being with me.

I appreciate the warmth of these encounters. I will switch to other people if I don't sense a good personal connection. When I have an appointment, I actually look forward to seeing them as friends. They are very nurturing to me. I need to feel that they are not just filling my cavities, prescribing medications, or figuring my deductions, but that they are kindred spirits. I want them to be glad to see me, and I want to feel emotionally enriched when I leave.

Because I'm self-employed, I meet with my accountant two or three times a year. He's this big, friendly teddy bear of a man. He smiles and fully acknowledges me when he first sees me in his waiting room, and he pulls me up onto my feet by grasping my hands. He's extremely bright and helps me make sense of taxes and finances that are ordinarily overwhelming to me. He gives me a warm hug on the way out, and I feel satisfied each time I depart. We get the accounting job done with good humor and mutual respect. I feel as though he is a wise father substitute who has my best interests at heart.

EXERCISE 42.   SEEK OUT FATHER SUBSTITUTES

As a child, you had no control over the way you were fathered. If your dad wasn't doing his job, you couldn't very well announce that you were going out to look for a better father! But as a grown up, there is a whole new world of stand-in dads to explore. Some of what you did not experience with your own father, you can receive from a variety of men in your current life.

You may find father-like support where you work or in your community from interested employers, teachers, or colleagues who are wiser or more experienced in some way than you are. Build your relationship with a substitute dad one step at a time. Father-wounded people often find a surrogate dad and want to hold onto him for dear life. Such dependency might overload the person and cause him to back away from you. Allowing yourself to have several mentors will moderate your tendency to take any one prisoner. Accept as much consideration as each adviser is willing to give.

Seek out father substitutes for yourself, men who are warm and encouraging. You can ask a male that you respect to be your mentor. A wide range of non-sexual, nurturing relationships is possible, from interactions with out-and-out adopted fathers to counselors to caring professionals to friendly acquaintances. They can model strength and effectiveness, while building your self-esteem through showing an interest in you.

Said a delighted female class member, "I'm so glad to have a name for what I'm doing – finding father substitutes. It gives me permission to look for the fathering I missed, and I can enjoy it so much more."

Deepening Your Experience

What could you use most from a surrogate dad? Specifically note down in your journal what you want and need. For example, you might write, "I'd like a mentor who will encourage me professionally." "I could use a father substitute who appreciates me as I am and enjoys my company." Or, "I'm looking for an ethical and spiritual adviser who can show me the correlation between my life and the 'big picture.'"

SHARING YOUR FATHER-WOUND

Communicating the truth about our father-loss with others has great value. As children, we probably adapted to a dysfunctional family by hiding our thoughts and feelings, becoming trapped behind denial and fear. As adults, we may try to protect ourselves from being hurt by disguising our sense of abandonment and shame. We fear being rejected if people perceive our neediness. We tend to see people as more powerful, more "together" than we are. We try to package ourselves to look good to everyone, even our closest friends.

Because we never know how individuals will respond, sharing about our father-wound is risky. When we permit special people to discern what is deep within, it brings us closer to them. Conveying our isolation and pain helps release the power of these feelings over us.

A well-known doctor, who is an excellent public speaker, always begins his talks by explaining how frightened he feels in front of an audience. If he tries to conceal his fear, he becomes even more nervous, lest his listeners discover his "weakness." Admitting his apprehension reduces its effect. As we acknowledge what limited, flawed, and fragile beings we are, we can give up the pretense that we must be capable, competent, and in control all the time. Truthfulness cuts through the shame.

My client Lisa worried that she might alienate her husband if she shared how often she felt lonely while he wasn't around. When he came home after she expected, she would give him the cold shoulder all evening to cover up her hurt and anger. We discussed how she was allowing her fear and self-doubt to control her and sabotage her chances of getting her needs met. The next time her husband was late, Lisa told him how alone she felt. He responded with understanding. The rest of the night, they had a wonderful time playing Scrabble, eating popcorn, and talking about the times each of them had felt lonely in the past. Lisa brought her husband closer by speaking her feelings, instead of being held hostage by them. She also asked him to routinely let her know ahead of time when he needed to be late so she would feel less abandoned.

Sharing our histories and reactions breaks us out of the fixed cycle of isolation and secrecy. We need to ask ourselves: Do we have friends we can open up to? From whom can we request emotional support? Is there anyone we can let see us cry?

When we make known our father-wound, we give ourselves the opportunity to find out which persons in our lives accept us as we are. Are they interested in our troubled feelings? Are they non-judgmental? Do they reciprocate by being unguarded with us? In hearing about others' difficulties, we see how much we have in common with them and how universal insecurities are. We may choose to surround ourselves only with those people who are able to be honest with us. As our capacity for intimacy increases, so will our circle of companions who desire genuine closeness.

EXERCISE 43.   REVEAL FATHER-LOSS

Even people who love each other do not automatically share the intimate details of their family backgrounds. Those of you who have previously discussed your past with partners may now have new insights regarding father-loss. One effective way to break out of the bind of holding everything inside is to talk in depth about your history to someone you trust.

Ask your mate and/or a close friend to meet especially to discuss about your past with your father. Go for a walk together, to a quiet restaurant, or just stay home - wherever you won't be interrupted. If sharing about yourself is unfamiliar or difficult for you, let your companion know this.

Relate a series of key incidents that reveal your father-wound. Explain what your dad was like and how he affected you. Communicate feelings as well as facts. Describe to the other person what you have learned about your upbringing and your makeup as a result of working on healing from your inadequate fathering.

Reveal your pain, fears, and shame slowly, like peeling the layers of an onion. If you are concerned about your friend's response, ask for a reaction. It may put you more at ease if s/he tells you about the struggles s/he has gone through as well.

Rich and Loretta had been married for four years. They held great affection for each other, yet both felt mistrust within the relationship. Rich told Loretta small lies that he believed sheltered her from unpleasantness. Detecting these fibs intensified her worries that he might be seeing another woman. They both threatened to separate frequently. They were uncomfortable making disclosures about their painful early life experiences.

Through an exchange of family stories, Loretta discovered that Rich, the eldest son, had to take care of his mother and siblings in place of an often absent father. He felt his role was to protect Loretta, even if it meant withholding specifics from her. For her part, she found it hard to believe that Rich could be faithful to her, since her father openly cheated on her mother. After listening to Loretta describe her fears and hurts resulting from her father-loss, Rich finally understood that Loretta would only tolerate hearing him tell the complete truth.

This heartfelt interchange released much of the tension between them. They saw how deep-seated suspicions and insecurities from their past fueled their current conflicts. The added perspective helped them to not overreact to unintended slights. Knowing the context of their particular backgrounds greatly increased the compassion they had for each other.

THE FATHER-LOSS RELATIONSHIP SYNDROME

We father-wounded people strongly tend to bring a specific set of patterns to relationships. The behaviors and attitudes that we learned in childhood often make it hard to achieve what we want the most when we grow up: to come close to other human beings. Once we understand and accept why we act and react as we do, we definitely have the power to make changes in the way we relate.

As youngsters, it was appropriate to turn to our fathers for nurturing and protection. Unfortunately, too many of us did not get what we needed from them. As adults, we are likely to continue to wish for other persons to fill our empty spaces, believing that our happiness depends on being accepted and loved. Yet no one else can make us whole.

We may yearn for love but not feel worthy of it. When we are desperate, we might settle for mere sexual gratification or for being with someone who is not right for us because we think we don't deserve better. We tend to seek from others what we feel we lack in ourselves. We hope our partners will make up for the deficiency and hurt we experienced with our dads. We tell ourselves that our mates should have the ability to make us feel complete.

We feel inadequate, so we look to our companions to give us security, status, relief from being alone, and the sense that we are cherished. Then we feel we owe them something in return. We may have sex when we don't want to or do favors out of obligation. We end up feeling resentful.

Our childhood wounds tend to cause us to repeat patterns with our significant others that we established much earlier with our dads. Insufficient fathering often leaves us so preoccupied with our own pain and needs that we have little energy left over to be emotionally available to a beloved. Having never experienced bonding and nurturing from a dad, we are liable to pick intimates who create in us the same feelings we had as youngsters. Deprivation may seem to us an inescapable adjunct to love.

A father-loss *man* frequently has not learned how to interact with women in an equitable and kind manner. This results from not seeing his father treat his mother with affection and respect. When dad was distant with his children, he most likely was not loving with his wife, either. The example of his father ignoring, demeaning, even abusing his mom can produce in a son patterns that are difficult to break. Opening himself to emotional closeness is difficult because he never experienced it with his own family.

An inadequately fathered *woman* often makes unrealistic demands on her partner. She maintains fantasies of being totally supported, protected, and valued. She tends to idealize her mate, then becomes disappointed when he doesn't live up to her expectations. Disillusioned, she dreams of another man who will make her happy. These imaginings come from a deep wish to finally find a father figure who will love her.

A father-loss woman has difficulty trusting her beloved. She doubts she is lovable, so she continually seeks reassurance or questions her man's devotion. She also has an exaggerated fear of abandonment and rejection. This makes her cling dependently to a partner or hold onto an unsatisfactory relationship far too long.

Some father-wounded women actually have generous and loving mates, but they are so mistrustful that they won't allow themselves to accept what is close-at-hand. One woman workshop participant said, "I can't feel sure that my partner will be there for me. In fact, I won't let him be there, because even if I believe he is today, he might leave me tomorrow. And I can't risk that, so I keep him at arm's distance." Other women push away solid men in favor of ones who act similarly to their dysfunctional dads.

The good news is that healing our father-loss will improve our close relationships. The more we are aware of the kind of bonding we had with our

fathers when we were children, and the more we clear away past hurt, guilt, and resentment, the greater are our possibilities for making high quality connections today.

We do not have to live with the discouragement that we experienced earlier in our lives. We are not required to replicate with others what happened with our dads. We have the capacity to either right the relationship we're in or prepare ourselves for the right relationship.

For single father-loss people, the period between romances can feel anxious and unsatisfying. We may believe that once someone adores us, then we'll feel good about ourselves. Yet it actually works the other way around. Loving ourselves as we are enables us to find a companion who treasures us. Self-appreciation creates a contented inner glow that draws others to us.

EXERCISE 44. WHAT I WANT IN A MATE

What are you looking for in a new beloved or in the one you have? Trying to define your specifications more closely can keep you from setting impossible standards. You are likelier to get what you desire by clearly declaring your intentions. You might also reflect on what capacities you need to develop to make yourself into a better companion. Carefully considering what you want in a beloved can give you clues as to where you feel deficient.

Write a list of ten qualities you would like in a potential mate. If you're already in a relationship, identify characteristics you appreciate most or would like to see more of in your current partner. Do this before you read further.

One class member compiled the following inventory.

I would like my mate to have:

1. Self-love

2. Self-confidence

3. Physical and emotional strength

4. Gentleness

5. A sense of humor

6. Empathy

7. A willingness to listen

8. Respect and love for family

9. A good-paying and enjoyable job

10. Honesty

You naturally want your present or future companion to be a wonderful person with many fine virtues. Most likely, you have an underlying hope as well: "I want my beloved to be everything I am not and have everything I don't have." Seeking the perfect mate is like looking for your missing dad all over again.

You can use this register of "partner qualities" to help you claim your own power. The traits you wish for in your significant other are precisely those you need to foster in yourself in order to feel complete.

Go back over your list. But use it as a guide to the attributes you need to develop in your relationship with *yourself*. Focus your attention back on you. For example, if what you say you want in your mate is "honesty," reconsider this statement as showing the need to develop truthfulness with *yourself*. You might interpret some of the characteristics in the above list as showing: "I would do well to treat *myself* with more 'gentleness,' I could build up *my own* 'physical and emotional strength,' and *I* could show more 'respect and love for family.'" Write out comparable statements describing each of your ten desired features in terms of yourself.

For every trait, go on to think about one way you would act differently if you emphasized that attribute in yourself. You could note that if you had additional "self-confidence," you would carry on business phone calls more assuredly. If you allowed yourself a lighter "sense of humor," you would laugh when you misplaced items, instead of getting angry at yourself. Or if you had a greater "willingness to listen," you would trust your intuition more.

In addition, what negative tendencies could you relinquish, if you accentuated these characteristics in yourself? For example, you might say to yourself, "If I had more 'empathy' for myself, then I would no longer need to act like a victim to get attention." Or, "If I got a 'good-paying job,' then I would no longer have to operate as though my mate had most of the power and the right to make our major decisions."

Now finish a similar sentence for all ten of the qualities that you enumerated: "If I had more... myself, then I would no longer need to..."

Once you fill in the holes left by your damaging fathering, you will find yourself seeking a more balanced relationship with your partner. As you grow, your mate will evolve too. When you are open to, intimate with, and committed to yourself, then you will attract the kind of person who is ready for a mature connection.

It is easy to hope that your partner will fulfill your dreams. But your sweetheart is not responsible for your happiness – you are. Rather than trying to change your significant other, concentrate on yourself. When you love yourself more, you might realize that the mate you already have offers all you can reasonably expect from another person.

YOUR LOVER IS YOUR MIRROR

We can see our reflection in our partners. The persons we choose to love and be with provide a way for us to identify our gifts and failings, if we are willing to look at these attributes. Intimates who appreciate and believe in us bring out our best. Like an improving mirror, they call on us to fulfill our potential. At the same time, what we dislike in our mates shows us aspects of ourselves we may routinely disclaim.

Relationships provide an ideal means of self-discovery. Those qualities that most bug us about our counterparts call attention to the very traits in ourselves where we are unresolved, fearful, still hurting. When we wag our fingers in condemnation, we reveal the truth: while one finger points out at them, three point back at us! Our reactions to their behaviors expose our own unsettled, touchy areas.

During conflicts, it's comforting to pretend that the cause of the trouble is "over there" – their problem, not ours. But we cannot separate ourselves from

our mates, our "other halves." This is as fruitless an enterprise as trying to cut off noses we don't like. Our intimates hold up mirrors that reveal our unacknowledged dark sides. What we hide from ourselves, the people closest to us will display to us. What we suppress, they'll express. For example, if our companions have temper tantrums, then some part of us carries secret rage, despite our seeming composure. Our significant others lay bare our deepest wounds, and we theirs.

When John and Claire met, he was apparently confident and successful. She was frequently needy and moody. John felt good about himself for taking care of Claire when she was depressed. After several years of marriage, John's hidden regret over his lost opportunities and his pessimism about the future surfaced. But instead of seeing that Claire was in fact acting out his own deepest fears and attitudes, he continued to criticize her for being weak and negative. They ultimately divorced.

Separating from specific partners cannot rid us of our nature. We will only find others who bring up similar issues for us to deal with. Looking hard at what we disapprove of in our mates clarifies what we have to accept or modify internally. They disclose us to ourselves. What we cannot easily see looking within, they put in front of our faces, inviting us to confront ourselves rather than deny our reality.

MAKING ARGUMENTS WORK FOR YOU

Even when both partners conscientiously own their issues, conflicts are virtually inevitable. Once you work through disagreements, you have confidence that you can survive other problems. The enduring strength of a relationship depends on the participants' willingness to tell each other the truth. They need to look for the internal source of the troubled feelings their interaction brings up. A searching honesty grounds the connection and keeps it real. To float on a cloud of love and contentment is wonderful; to know that you can have disputes, *learn from them,* and then return to the softness of affection is even better.

You can understand a great deal about yourself by investigating the deeper reasons you get upset at someone close to you. Fights open a window to view yourself more clearly. It is easy to get lost in details or in blaming your counterpart. Focusing on the flaws of the other person obscures your own failings. Quarrels are virtually never about the supposed subject. Their emotional charge reveals underlying fault lines you strive to conceal. Arguments project out feelings you normally disguise inside.

In every close friendship, people get angry with each other. Your companion's specific attitudes or behaviors trigger your internal "hot buttons." You may automatically react by feeling, "How could s/he do this to me?" Instead, you have the chance to treat your annoyance at the other person's conduct as an opportunity to expose and work through deeper levels of your own father-loss.

Heated strife and outrage usually indicate an overreaction: the intensity of your response is most likely greater than the present circumstance warrants. Let's say your beloved's actions make you mad. Perhaps s/he overdraws the bank account, arrives late for a date with you, or calls you by a crude name. You rant or stage an icy withdrawal. Even though your mate did do something that hurt you, your extreme reaction signals the touching of an old wound. The fury you feel is mostly about the past.

Father-loss people overreact to current pain because it reactivates unmended injuries. Only some ten percent of your feelings comes from the immediate stimulus. Your partner is probably triggering your sense of childhood neglect or abuse. With little basis in reality, you can feel trapped or abandoned. Communications specialist Steven Winer says that when you are extremely disturbed by an encounter, about fifty percent of your reaction is linked to traumas before the age of six and about forty percent to later events that replicate these original painful situations. Like the tip of an iceberg above the water line, present-day arguments connect to submerged former anger and pain.

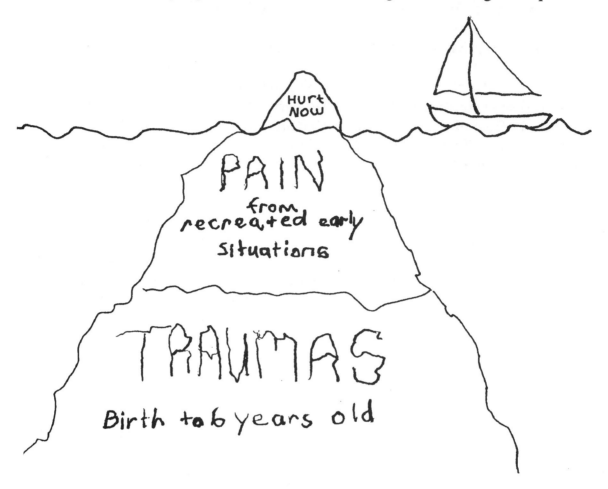

I remember taking a camping trip with my husband and two of his children from a previous marriage. The twelve-year-old forgot to bring her toothbrush. We were going for only two days, and my solution would have been for her to share her sister's, use her finger, or do without brushing. Instead, my husband made a special excursion into the nearest little town to buy her a new one. I was upset at the time by all the "fuss" made over a missing toothbrush. By sharing my feelings with him, I came to realize that deep-down I was hurt that no daddy ever fussed over me that way.

Triggering incidents can give you a clear picture and a dynamic access into the unfinished business of your father-loss. The strong emotions you express are a potential gold mine for healing, when you see their link to your past. Keep remembering that your mate is just the spark, not the source of your pain. In the middle of a dispute, if you are able to make the connection to earlier traumas, your overreactions can help you grow. Then you can begin to quit replaying the old dramas. Revelations that come with your adult understanding provide an opportunity to reorient outdated attitudes and reconstruct your emotional foundations.

INTIMATE RELATIONSHIPS CAN HEAL

Squabbles with people who are close to you provide an occasion for both parties to better understand their primal motivations and you to find greater resolution of your father-loss. There is a specific technique you can use to make hot, contentious feelings work for you. You and your partner can sit down together, take turns exploring how your powerful emotions indicate an exaggerated reflex, and investigate the underlying sources of your pain.

Of course, in the middle of an intense encounter, it is difficult to achieve perspective. But you can train yourself to catch overreactions. You can stop, calm down, and start a dialogue. This is far better than saying words that you could regret later. If not during a spat, then as soon thereafter as possible, process what happened. The person who feels most stressed is the one who should begin speaking. Be sure to stay in touch with the full range of your sensations. Relax your body, be patient, and let your emotions surface. There are no wrong feelings. Trust that they will take you where you need to go.

Prepare your partner by admitting that there is a good chance you are overreacting, that s/he is merely the trigger, rather than the actual reason for your sharp pain. Indicate that your purpose in sharing is to understand your own responses, not to attack or control the other person. Only when you are sure that your listener is receptive and does not feel threatened, do you have a green light to communicate further.

Start talking about what you believe bothered you during the current episode. Then let yourself remember a particular situation when you had similar feelings. As you recollect the details from that experience, allow yourself to embrace the intensity of the hurt that you felt at this earlier time. Let specific memories emerge until the "secret" comes out, an agonizing event that you are protecting yourself from recalling or admitting to another human being. It may be a shocking incident or a seemingly small moment that greatly affected you.

Achieving this kind of emotional release is pay dirt. The acute ache goes away when you reveal what you are hiding. As you dig up buried feelings, you'll see how your previous traumas have distorted your perceptions. Misreading other people's intentions or expecting them to satisfy overwhelming needs both have the effect of sabotaging your present-day relationships. You can become clearer about what you would realistically like your partner to provide you now.

Scott found himself very unhappy with his friend Joan, because she waited several days before returning his repeated phone messages. He realized that she was just a trigger for his deep feelings and asked for the chance to share them with her. Scott admitted that as he waited for her to call back he felt abandoned by her. He began recalling specific situations from the past when he feared those he loved would desert him.

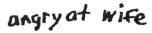

The first event he remembered was being drunk and verbally abusive with his new wife. She started running away from him. He panicked, fearing that she might ask for a divorce and never concern herself with him again. While relating this story, he re-experienced how unloved and worthless he had felt at that moment.

Scott went on to recollect an earlier and even more significant happening, when he was just three years old. His father was backing out of their driveway to go on a business trip. Hanging onto a juniper tree crying, Scott screamed, "Don't leave me! Don't leave me!" He felt that his father's departure meant dad didn't love him.

Then Scott called to mind that when he was two, a baby-sitter sexually abused him. He was frightened and felt out of control. This small boy made sense of the situation then by deciding that his parents had forsaken him and didn't care about him. At that young age, he determined that there was no one for him to depend on or trust.

When Scott finished telling Joan about these memories, he felt closer to her. He saw how little his reactions had to do with her actual behavior toward him. Anyone pulling away from him or not responding quickly to his overtures set off his deep-seated fear of abandonment. Scott gave himself the opportunity to go back to the original source of his feelings and release them. He came to a new conclusion about life to replace the incorrect one he had assumed as a toddler. In a series of positive affirmations, he communicated directly to his inner child that others do care about him, even when it looks to him at the moment as though they are intentionally rejecting him. He can do a "reality check" by considering carefully whether or not intimates are in fact deliberately distancing themselves from him.

Probing into incidents that trigger you may not result in as dramatic revelations as those Scott discovered. Apparently trivial childhood happenings can have deep effects that persist into adulthood. Don't be discouraged if you find it difficult to delve into early, painful experiences. Just let your mind wander back through the years, and certain scenes will arise. Becoming comfortable with this process takes time. Go easy and allow yourself to slowly get better at it.

The goal of sharing is to liberate you from your pain, not to manipulate your partner into meeting your needs. By spontaneously expressing your feelings, you can gain clarity and relief. When you acknowledge how your friend's present behavior is hooking you into your father-loss, it frees you from blaming him or her for your suffering. By taking the risk of exposing your innermost self, you may come to realize that your companion is able and willing to love, accept, and affirm you in ways your father never did.

EXERCISE 45. THE GIFT OF TRIGGERS

Three "Triggers"

What follows is a step-by-step procedure that you can undertake any time you find yourself having an overblown response during a dispute with a close friend. You can use such an occasion to probe deeply into the sources of your own emotional makeup. To produce the best results, you can adopt an especially receptive mode when your friend is sharing with you. You can also propose a way for him or her to listen while you are expressing your feelings. One person at a time speaks The other person is an active listener, who lets go of any personal agendas to give full attention to understanding the other.

Try these guidelines during the next crisis or blowup you have with your mate or a good friend. You could also go back over your last argument and apply these principles retroactively to gain greater clarity.

As the upset person:

1. When you see that you are irritated and reacting strongly, realize your distress is only partially about your friend. S/he is just the trigger, not the source of your feelings.

2. Ask for permission to talk about why you believe you responded so forcefully. Reassure your listener by admitting that s/he is responsible for only a small percentage of your distress. In this way, your communication is not so threatening. You might say, "I want to share my reactions with you in a non-attacking way. I don't want you to feel hurt. I want you to know that being close to you is very important to me. I want this to work out."

3. Tell your companion that you need to talk about your reactions in order to understand your own feelings and the root of your pain.

4. Begin by sharing your feelings. Allow your immediate distress to lead you back to memories of previous traumas. Talk about a specific situation from the past when you experienced a similar emotion, such as feeling abandoned, frightened, or betrayed. Keep recalling related memories until you reach the earliest time you had that feeling. Some of these recollections will connect back to your father-wound.

5. Do your best to remember what negative judgments or decisions about life, yourself, and others you might have made at the time of these traumas. People have reported telling themselves: "I'll never trust anyone again… I don't need anyone… I can do everything by myself… I'll show you… It's better not to take risks… I'm not good enough… I'll always be alone."

6. In the presence of your friend, make new declarations to your inner child. The determinations you made as a youngster were often inaccurate and self-defeating. Draw different conclusions at this time, ones that work positively for you. For example, affirm that "I will trust people until they prove themselves unreliable… I am good enough… I want to let special people get close to me… I am friendly and open… I like to include others in my plans."

7. Allow your companion to respond genuinely. Love depends on support freely given, not extracted. When you are candid, without demanding a particular proof of caring, you are most likely to receive a response that pleases you.

As the listener:

1. Concentrate on the growth of your partner. Remember, a large part of his or her reaction had little to do with you. You simply set off the other person's underlying emotions.

2. Relax, breathe deeply, and be open to your feelings so you can reflect back what you believe is going on inside your companion. Receive what s/he is saying and feeling, doing your best to keep your own attitudes out of the dialogue.

3. Simply mirror your friend's emotions rather than intellectualizing, labelling, diagnosing, or problem-solving. Try using phrases such as "I sense that you feel..." or "What I hear you saying is..." Your role is to empathize and to be a witness to the person's self-discovery.

Being receptive and concerned when your partner needs to work through feelings is fundamental to maintaining an open and loving relationship. Still, it can be scary when an intimate expresses strong emotions. Don't rescue, analyze, or give advice, because these behaviors are ways to avoid your own feelings. As the listener, your job is simply to support the speaker's getting in touch with his or her feelings. When you don't take outbursts personally, you enable your companion to assume full responsibility for any reactions to your triggering behavior.

Detaching from the passionate feelings of an argument while your friend works through past hurt is not always easy. It requires a conscious decision to set aside your own feelings in order to be supportive of the other person. However, there may be occasions when you are unwilling to listen to another probe into old wounds because of your own pain. If this happens, be honest. Let your partner know that you care, but that at this moment it would be difficult for you to listen with an open mind. Suggest another time when you might be more emotionally available.

Deepening Your Experience

Whenever you try this technique, write down in your journal any primal traumas you discovered while you were sharing your response to your companion's triggering behavior. Was this information new to you, or had you made the connection before? What affirmations did you create to reprogram your inner child? Were you able to more readily resolve the original conflict with your friend after you addressed your internal issues?

EXERCISE 46. YOUR BELOVED'S INNER CHILD

Inside everyone is a wounded child. As an adult, you may be accustomed to ignoring this hurting, needy little person. Yet your inner child is an active participant in most intimate interactions, whether or not you acknowledge this side of yourself. Buried amid the feelings stirred up by arguments with those you love, you will generally find two kids who are scared of rejection and abandonment. An important part of healing your intimate relationships is to nurture each other's inner children.

Untangling childhood needs from their adult expression will de-escalate most intense encounters. For example, Carol and John lived together but were fighting so much they decided to move into separate rooms. One evening, John seemed trouble and retired early. Carol later knocked on his door, went over to him, and wordlessly rocked and stroked him. He started crying, telling her how much he didn't want to lose her. Meeting the needs of John's scared inner child dissolved the distance between them. It is not yet clear if their relationship will survive, but in the meantime they are able to nourish one another while openly discussing their preferences and their pain.

This exercise is not just for romantic partners. You can undertake it with people of the same sex in brotherly or sisterly comradeship. Because it is not erotic, you can also practice it with opposite sex friends, so long as you keep the focus on comforting the child within.

One way to connect with your partner's inner child is to show him or her how lovable s/he is through tender, nurturing touch, like a mother rocking a youngster with a stomachache, or a father reading to his little one.

Invite your companion to sit or lie down, perhaps putting his or her head in your lap. Just hold the person, while nonverbally communicating your caring. You could gently

stroke the hair, forehead, and cheeks. Be careful to avoid erotic caresses. Concentrate instead on being like a concerned adult who is soothing the needy yet precious child that lives inside your partner's grown-up body. Other areas to rub or pat are the back, shoulders, stomach, and feet. You might like to have peaceful instrumental music playing in the background. After a time, switch places and allow your friend to comfort you.

For those of you whose father-wounds include physical abuse, accepting nourishing touch can seem very threatening. Proceed slowly. Your tendency may be to give but not to receive. You too deserve nurturing, and your inner child can learn that stroking does not have to involve sexuality or molestation. Set any boundaries that you might need in order to feel secure. Identify the safest areas to have touched and begin there. Even limited contact may feel uncomfortable, but tell the child inside you that it is good to be consoled by someone who loves you.

If you are the partner embracing an individual who has been physically or sexually abused, judiciously respect declared limits and keep your contact nonsexual. You don't want to reaffirm that erotic touch is the only nurturing s/he can ever receive. Even a hint of sexuality could trigger old traumas and cause your counterpart to shut down or pull away.

You and your friend can share this nonverbal stroking at any time. Initiating such holding can be particularly valuable whenever either person is distraught. You can stop in the middle of an unpleasant dispute and realize that your two inner kids need to be cherished, accepted, and nourished. Underlying fears of being rejected and abandoned respond well to the reassurance of a gentle touch. Often the true nature of the conflict has to do with a perceived lack of recognition and caring, rather than the matter superficially at issue.

Your mate's inner child operates on a physical and emotional plane rather than a mental one. Sensible logic doesn't count for much. Pay attention to the senses and feelings first, then talk. Satisfying your deep yearnings to be esteemed and valued creates harmony between you.

Deepening Your Experience

Little kids are prone to take emotional responsibility for what is not their fault. Similarly, inner children need to know whether or not they are the cause of their partner's moods. Consider giving your relationship a name of its own, such as "Serenity" or "Paradise." By so doing, you can differentiate your own and your mate's difficult times from the condition of the relationship. You might say to your companion, "You seem tired and unhappy today. But how is Serenity?" The answer could be, "I've had a really hard day, but Serenity is fine!," or "I'm unhappy, and the problem is Serenity. Maybe we better talk about what's bothering me."

Playing with the kid inside your mate can be a lot of fun. Try bowling, skating, go-cart racing, or other lively activities.

Take time to appreciate the tender child within your partner through small notes of appreciation tucked away in pockets or clothing drawers.

A father-loss person needs compassionate understanding more than anything else. The following guidelines can help you and your companion communicate better and reach greater depths of intimacy. Share this information with those who are closest to you. It will convey to them how best to interact with you to fulfill your special needs. Phrased as a direct address to them rather than you, I have printed these suggestions on separate pages, so you can readily make copies. Virtually everything in this tipsheet is good advice for a friend as well as a beloved, even though the specific reference is to a romantic relationship.

TIPS FOR FRIENDS AND LOVERS OF THE FATHER-WOUNDED

• Many of your partner's problems stem from damaging experiences with his or her father. Seeing this connection between present behavior and past injuries will make it easier for you to be understanding and tolerant. If you can realize that you, too, have inner wounds that need healing, you may be able to be more accepting of your companion's difficulties.

• Encourage your mate to talk about his or her father. Listen closely to your beloved's descriptions of earlier troubling experiences. Sometimes when s/he is hurting, you could say, "I can see you are in pain right now. Could this have something to do with how you've felt about your dad?" S/he may be able to help you make similar insights about your father. If your mate is not receptive to your probing, you needn't press the issue. Perhaps your timing is off or you are mistaken. You may just be planting seeds that will produce revelations at a later time.

• Understand that your beloved may fear abandonment and have greater than ordinary needs for reassurance, resulting in exaggerated worries about losing you. Resist getting upset in response to this hypersensitivity. Add in your point of view, so s/he grasps that there is more than one possible interpretation of your actions. See whether you can identify together the behaviors or circumstances that tend to trigger your mate's insecurity alarm. Then work out and agree to follow clear protocols for how you can reduce potential misunderstandings in the future. For example, if your being punctual is important to your partner, you can make a commitment to faithfully call whenever you are going to be late.

• Encourage your mate to put feelings into words. His or her father probably wasn't available to be interactive or to show much of himself. When your partner shares about what s/he experienced growing up, show that you empathize with his or her distress. One way you can bring about greater openness is to talk freely about your own upbringing.

• Be openly expressive about your reactions to your companion. Often father-wounded people had to guess what their dads felt because they received unclear messages. Your forthright feedback can offset doubts about where you stand at any moment, promoting a trust in your authenticity.

• Do what you say. Though important in every relationship, dependability is even more crucial for you, since your beloved probably couldn't count on dad keeping his promises.

• Be as available as you can when your mate needs to express anger, fear, and even suspicion toward you. Listen carefully to this sharing. Understand that many of your partner's concerns derive from the past. You needn't take them all personally. If reactions seem unfounded, or only remotely related to the present situation, then you can encourage your mate to reach deep within to find the original sources of the upset. Talking about former traumas can help release the hold of these old experiences. Be sure to ask, "Is that everything, or do you have more to say?" It's best to get all the feelings out in order to clear the air.

• Set boundaries that are right for you. Your partner may make subtle demands on you to be the father s/he always wanted. Since you can never be this idealized dad, let your mate know what to realistically expect from you and what you will not deliver. Be true to yourself.

• Frequently voice your approval and respect toward your loved one. Don't assume s/he knows of your love and caring. You can't satisfy all the needs and desires that come from father-loss, but you can let your partner know in what ways s/he is important to you. Make sure s/he also states appreciation of you.

• Demonstrate your affection. Occasionally give tangible indicators of your caring, such as small gifts, delightful surprises, and frequent notes that convey the depth of your feelings.

• If your loved one has a tendency to withdraw from social interactions, notice if the two of you isolate from others as a couple. If so, emphasize relationships with friends and encourage your mate to participate fully in them.

• As you assist in your partner's work on healing the father-wound, you might find it helpful to apply some the lessons s/he is learning to your own life. Openly and sensitively dealing with the effects of inadequate fathering can lead you to a deeper, more intimate connection and bring greater joy in your time together.

MUTUAL AFFIRMATION

Our progress toward healing has enabled us to more easily acknowledge the good in ourselves. Now it's time to apply this accepting attitude to our mates. Father-loss tends to produce a focus on the negative. If dad often undercut our self-esteem, we may feel insecure and easily slip into the habit of berating our companions as well as ourselves.

One effective means to counteract habitual criticalness is to make a point of voicing appreciation. It is important to constantly bear witness to the positive in ourselves and in our beloveds. As we express the good we experience in our mates, we encourage the very qualities we admire. In return, they will probably emphasize the virtues they see in us. Mutual affirmation creates a warm and nurturing environment. It becomes easier to develop those parts of the relationship that work well and to take pleasure in our special bond.

EXERCISE 47.   SIMPLY APPRECIATE

It's tempting to take a loved one's favorable traits for granted. You assume his or her good points as a given, but anything more than mere coexistence deserves credit. Beneficial qualities are a gift. If your companion routinely acts graciously toward you, this is all the more reason to be thankful.

The best way to get more of what you like from your significant other is to acknowledge what s/he is already giving you. Recognition also builds your partner's self-esteem. The better your counterpart feels about him or her self, the brighter energy s/he will bring to your relationship. You likewise glow more when you reflect the radiance in your beloved.

As in all the relationship exercises, you can practice the following with either a close friend or a lover, of the same or opposite sex.

Light a candle to make this caring ritual a special time. Play mellow music that you both enjoy. Sit across from your companion. Look into each other's eyes.

Start by expressing what you like and appreciate about the other person. Mention at least three attributes or behaviors.

Sample statements include: "One thing I love about you is how you wake up so cheerful every morning." "I appreciate how kind you are to my parents." "I like your soft, gentle voice." If you are feeling especially affectionate toward your partner, keep going as long as you please.

After you have made this exchange of mutual appreciations, you can go on to state your gratitude for specific actions your companion has taken on your behalf in the recent past. For example, you could note, "When you went out of your way to pick up my dry cleaning, so I wouldn't have to make an extra trip, I really felt how much you care about me and want to make me happy." Let each other know how much pleasure your small favors bring.

Continue by indicating at least two actions you promise to make to show your satisfaction at having this partner in your life. You could pledge to provide a full body massage within the week or to serve breakfast in bed.

Finally, brainstorm about how you two could have some especially fun times. Discuss what you might do with each other that would make you both feel genuinely good. Identify what activities to add to your customary routines that would bring more pleasure into your life together, such as daily walks, playing sports, or having friends over for dinner more often.

You can regularly schedule this exercise or undertake it whenever the atmosphere between you becomes either particularly flat or turbulent. All relationships have trying times. The deliberate voicing of mutual admiration and respect reminds you why you spend time with this person and what you love about him or her.

Deepening Your Experience

Write a letter to your partner expressing your appreciation of who s/he is and how s/he enhances your life.

ENCOURAGING EACH OTHER'S DREAMS

We father-wounded people have a tendency to surrender too much of our self-direction to our partners, in hopes that they will take care of most of our needs. Often we want more than any other person can provide. We routinely stifle our own aims and creativity for the sake of our relationships. Then we feel disappointed, cheated, and lonely for the parts of ourselves that we gave up for the good of the connections.

How many of us had positive models of balanced, mutually supportive unions between our parents? In contrast, were we shown how to martyr ourselves for our companions? Did either or both of our folks relinquish dreams for the other? The basis of a successful relationship is two self-sustaining individuals joining together into one exclusive bond which helps each to fulfill his or her vision in life.

Even in loving partnerships, we need an independent sense of purpose outside the pairing. Resisting the inclination to sacrifice for our mates, we can instead strengthen companionships by both persons sharing the excitement of struggling to realize personal goals. Being enthusiastic about our mates' missions in life confirms that we fit together as couples.

We reinforce our loved ones by expressing our confidence in their capacities to realize their ideals. If they can't look to us to believe in them, who will? One measure of whether our relationships are working well is how much we stay in touch with and progress toward achieving our own dreams. Love involves accepting the other persons exactly as they are, facilitating clarity about their fondest desires, and feeling free to follow our inner stars.

Dan and Susan, married for thirty years with three children, are exemplary for their willingness to let each other pursue their dreams. Dan was first a military and then a test pilot. While Susan was frightened at the danger inherent in this line of work, she understood that Dan had to fly in order to feel fulfilled. For his part, when Susan settled on real estate as a career, Dan had to spend many evenings and weekends without her. They consistently gave each other encouragement to achieve their aims. Supporting ourselves and our partners to attain our highest intentions as human beings elevates connections from the merely satisfying toward the sublime.

EXERCISE 48.   VALIDATE YOUR VISIONS

The best imaginable scenario is having a companion who inspires you to find and follow your authentic path in order to achieve your potential. Love encourages you to realize your highest purpose. You in turn can enhance your significant other's self-confidence and pursuit of his or her vision.

This exercise is about manifesting your deepest desires. It is not about the past but the future, not about old pain but current fulfillment. Receiving support and inspiration to accomplish your dreams is transforming. This process will work as well with friends and family members as mates.

Set aside a quiet time for you and your partner to be together. Put on soothing music. Sit across from each other. Begin by describing three visions that motivate and inspire you. For example, you might say – with as much elaboration as you feel is appropriate:

1. I've always wanted to sing. I would like to take voice lessons and join a chorus that performs in front of audiences.

2. What's really important to me is that my work help others. I'd like to find a new career where I primarily give service.

3. I have a vision of traveling to Japan to visit temples and shrines to gain a deeper spiritual sense.

The listener responds, "I visualize you manifesting your dreams." S/he narrates back the vision using the speaker's own words plus added details, saying for example, "I can see you in Japan. You are in a tranquil temple where you feel spiritually uplifted and renewed." Then the second person communicates his or her ideals and receives the partner's reinforcing feedback. Sharing your dreams and hearing them repeated makes them seem more concrete.

Now look deeply into the eyes of your friend, as though you were seeing all the way into the soul. While intensely gazing at each other, retain your confidant's visions in your mind's eye. Keep beholding and communing silently for several minutes.

Each of you then can audibly give thanks to your Spiritual Father for helping you fulfill your respective goals. Think of each of your dreams as already an accomplished reality.

Trust that you can bring your ideals into being, that they are being realized right now. Know that you can count on the support of the Universe to attain your highest destiny.

Reenact this process as often as you feel moved.

Deepening Your Experience

You can help each other progress from envisioning your dreams toward manifesting them. Like a good dad might have done, you and your partner can spend several sessions outlining the potential steps necessary to reach your individual visions. List all the stages from first to last you must pass through to achieve realization.

Do monthly updates to ascertain how much you've accomplished and what remains to be done in order to keep each of your dreams moving toward fulfillment.

THE HERO/INE'S JOURNEY

Embarking on an inner journey to find out who we are has taken heroic courage. Despite our backgrounds with our fathers, our sense of innate value and purpose led us to undertake this quest. Moving through the exercises in this book has brought us into unknown territory. Our reward has been release and revelation. From here, we can look forward rather than backward. Settling old resentments regarding our dads has put more of our past at peace. We can now recognize the strength, insight, and compassion we have gained from coming through our father-loss trauma.

We have done battle with mighty dragons. At first we may believe that our dads themselves are the creatures that we must conquer. They are not! Our dragons are inside us. They comprise the dark parts of ourselves that push us to be fearful and blaming. We can feel proud for having met our monsters head on. We've begun to soften them with love and understanding, to disarm them by accepting responsibility for our own behavior and circumstances.

From an adult perspective, we can see that most fathers are not ogres – just fault-filled men. By perceiving their actual dimensions, we give them a manageable importance and influence in our lives. We can now separate the specific actions of our dads, about which we can do nothing, from their effects on our inner states and outer conduct, about which we can do a great deal.

We are not alone on this adventure. All those who have endured inadequate fathering accompany us. We have the opportunity to share about our father-wounds in support groups or with trusted friends and mates. Emerging from our trials empowered, we can convey to others what we have learned.

Healing father-loss brings us closer to accepting our humanity and to unconditionally loving ourselves and others. Self-esteem is the key to happiness and the best basis for finding and sustaining good relationships. Of course, we have further work to do, but we are clearly worthwhile people just as we are. No matter what deprivation or desperation we have experienced, we can at last acknowledge that we have been and always will be *enough*.

I commend you for having made it through to the end of this workbook. You and I have undergone a far-reaching voyage together, forming a real bond of trust and mutual respect. Now it is time to say good-bye. Having learned a great deal, you're ready to graduate, to continue on your own, though you may want to periodically go back and redo the exercises that were particularly meaningful to you.

Commencements are a rite of passage that proclaim you have completed a milestone in your life. Coming to terms with your father represents a landmark of emotional maturity. You have reason to celebrate.

I like to end my classes with an appreciation circle. Everyone forms together into an intimate ring, arms around shoulders. Members look directly at those in the group who particularly touched them and express thanks for their making themselves vulnerable and sharing their innermost selves.

You and I can do a similar round of acknowledgments now. I want to applaud you for having participated in this course in healing your father-wound. You have worked hard. From my own experience, I know how much self-discipline it has taken to apply yourself. I am glad to have had this opportunity to serve you. I put a great deal of thought and care into making this guidebook as useful and accessible as I possibly could. Your gaining so much from it makes my labors worthwhile.

For your part, you can appreciate the many seminar participants whose stories and comments I have shared throughout. You may feel you've gotten to know them, just as though you went through an intensive workshop with them. You can also be grateful for any encouragement you might have received from family, friends, a counselor, or a support group. Please especially thank those who discussed with you their memories and feelings about your dad.

I hope that you incorporate the tools you have gained here into your everyday life. My parting wish is that you keep making this book work for you, and that as a result you experience ever more fulfillment and joy.

NATIONAL SELF-HELP GROUPS

Alcoholics Anonymous
(Thousands of chapters are located
throughout the world. Check your
telephone book for local listings.)

Al-Anon Family Groups
1600 Corporate Landing Parkway
Virginia Beach, VA 23454-5617
(800) 344-2666

Adult Children of Alcoholics
P.O. Box 3216
Torrance, CA 90510
(310) 534-1815

A.R.T.S. Anonymous
(Artists Recovering through
           the Twelve Steps)
P.O. Box 175 Ansonia Station
New York, NY 10023
(212) 873-7075

CO-Dependents Anonymous
P.O. Box 33577
Phoenix, AZ 85067-3577
(602) 277-7991

Family Resource Coalition
200 South Michigan Ave. 16th Floor
Chicago, IL 60604
(312) 341-0900

Incest Survivors Anonymous
P.O. Box 17245
Long Beach, CA 90807-7245
(310) 428-5599

Narcotics Anonymous
P.O. Box 4143
Panorama City, CA 91412
(818) 997-3822

Overeaters Anonymous
World Service Office
P.O. Box 44020
Rio Rancho, NM 87174-4020
(505) 891-2664

Parents Anonymous
675 Foothill Blvd.
Clarement, CA 91711
(909) 621-6184

Sex and Love Addicts Anonymous
P.O. Box 650010
West Newton, MA 02165-0010
(617) 332-1845

Sexaholics Anonymous
P.O. Box 300
Simi Valley, CA 93062
(818) 704-9854

Survivors of Incest Anonymous
P.O. Box 21817
Baltimore, MD 21222-6817
(410) 282-3400

Tough Love
P.O. Box 1069
Doylestown, PA 18901
(215) 348-7090

RECOMMENDED READING

Beattie, Melody. *Codependent No More: How to Stop Controlling Others and Start Caring for Yourself.* New York: Harper/Hazelden, 1987.

Bloomfield, Harold H., et al. *Making Peace with Your Parents.* New York: Random House, 1983.

Bradshaw, John. *Healing the Shame That Binds You.* Deerfield Beach, Florida: Health Communications, 1988.

Farrell, Warren. *Why Men Are the Way They Are.* New York: McGraw-Hill, 1986.

Gawain, Shakti. *Living in the Light.* San Rafael, Calif.: Whatever Publishing, 1986.

Godwin, Gail. *Father's Melancholy Daughter.* New York: Morrow, 1991

Goulter, Barbara, and Joan Minninger. *The Father-Daughter Dance: Every Woman's Guide to the Key Male Relationship in Her Life.* New York: Avon, 1993.

Greer, Germaine. *Daddy, We Hardly Knew You.* New York: Knopf, 1990.

Leonard, Linda Schierse. *The Wounded Woman: Healing the Father-Daughter Relationship.* Boston: Shambhala Press, 1982.

Lerner, Harriet Goldhor. *The Dance of Anger: A Woman's Guide to Changing the Patterns of Intimate Relationships.* New York: Harper & Row, 1985.

Osherson, Samuel. *Finding Our Fathers: How a Man's Life Is Shaped by His Relationship with His Father.* New York: Fawcett Columbine, 1986.

Pittman, Frank. *Man Enough: Fathers, Sons, and the Search for Masculinity.* New York: Berkeley Publishing Group, 1993.

Scull, Charles. *Fathers, Sons, and Daughters.* Los Angeles: Jeremy P. Tarcher, 1992.

Secunda, Victoria. *Women and Their Fathers: The Sexual and Romantic Impact of the First Man in Your Life.* New York: Delacorte Press, 1992.

Smedes, Lewis B. *Forgive and Forget: Healing the Hurts We Don't Deserve.* San Francisco: Harper and Row, 1984.

Wakerman, Elyce. *Father Loss: Daughters Discuss the Man That Got Away.* New York: Doubleday, 1984.